MILWAUKEE GHOSTS

Sherry Strub

Schiffer Publishing Ltd

4880 Lower Valley Road, Atglen, Pennsylvania 19310

Dedication

To Craig and Nikki

Schiffer Books are available at special discounts for bulk purchases for sales promotions or premiums. Special editions, including personalized covers, corporate imprints, and excerpts can be created in large quantities for special needs. For more information contact the publisher:

Published by Schiffer Publishing Ltd.
4880 Lower Valley Road
Atglen, PA 19310
Phone: (610) 593-1777; Fax: (610) 593-2002
E-mail: Info@schifferbooks.com

For the largest selection of fine reference books on this and related subjects, please visit our web site at
www.schifferbooks.com
We are always looking for people to write books on new and related subjects.
If you have an idea for a book please contact us at the above address.

This book may be purchased from the publisher.
Include $3.95 for shipping.
Please try your bookstore first.
You may write for a free catalog.

In Europe, Schiffer books are distributed by
Bushwood Books
6 Marksbury Ave.
Kew Gardens
Surrey TW9 4JF England
Phone: 44 (0) 20 8392-8585; Fax: 44 (0) 20 8392-9876
E-mail: info@bushwoodbooks.co.uk
Website: www.bushwoodbooks.co.uk
Free postage in the U.K., Europe; air mail at cost.

Copyright © 2008 by Sherry Strub
Library of Congress Control Number: 2007941195

Designed by Mark David Bowyer
Type set in A Charming Font Super Expanded / NewBskvll BT

ISBN: 978-0-7643-2866-4
Printed in China

Contents

Acknowledgments

I'd like to thank my husband, Craig, for allowing me all the alone-time I needed to research and write this book. A big thanks to my daughter, Nikki, for not only allowing me to drag her along on my ghost investigations, but for being my biggest cheerleader and for proofreading my book in its early stages. Thanks to Mary Sutherland and Noah Voss, my paranormal experts, and all the great people who contributed true stories: especially Jim Aho, Diane Guell, Emmett Jordan, Kathy Orndorf, Trudy Blakely, and Ardith Ann Richter (and the others who wished to remain anonymous). Thank you Jennifer Salm and Sarah Simonson for joining me on one of my fact-finding missions/wild goose chases. It was a memorable day. Thank you, Sandra Beck, for being such a good friend and reading through my book before I sent it off, and Karen Laven, for your friendship and support from beginning to end. Lastly, I'd like to thank my parents, Audrey and George Ferkey, and all my brothers and sisters: George, Susan, Nancy, Danny, David, Lisa, Karla, Stacey, Jim, and Ken. And finally, a big thanks to Dinah Roseberry. I couldn't have asked for a better (and nicer!) editor.

Introduction
Brats, Beer, Brewers...and Ghosts

Most people, when asked what they think of when they hear the word "Milwaukee," might choose any of the following: brats, beer, Brewer's games at Miller Park, Harley-Davidson, Inc., the Milwaukee County Zoo, Summerfest...

But Milwaukee is also known for something else—its ghosts. Whether friendly or not so friendly, frightening or reassuring, Milwaukee and southeastern Wisconsin have lots of ghosts.

How did I arrive at this conclusion? Simple math. Milwaukee is a big city. Big cities have lots of people—and lots of deaths. And like it or not, death is usually the beginning of a ghost's existence.

If you ask an average Milwaukeean if he or she knows of a place in Milwaukee that's haunted, chances are excellent they will come up with at least one or two sites.

Do you believe in ghosts? Have you had an encounter with a spirit? Do others' ghostly experiences intrigue you?

You're not alone. According to a 2005 poll conducted by the Gallup Organization, approximately 32% of Americans believe ghosts do exist. Ghosts and the paranormal are more mainstream now than at any time in the past. It's almost impossible to go a day without hearing the word "ghost," seeing it in print, on a computer monitor, *TV*, or movie screen. I recently read a newspaper columnist's list of things she wanted to do before she died. One of them: spend the night alone in a haunted house.

Maybe you'd like to test your resolve and stay alone in a haunted house, or already have. Or maybe you're a believer like me who doesn't have the desire to get quite that friendly with a ghost. Whatever your interest in the spirit world, all you need to do is look at the number of paranormal TV shows, books, movies, and Web sites devoted to ghosts to know they're here to stay.

One thing I've learned along the way is that most ghosts like to hang out in old places. Milwaukee, rich in history, is glad to oblige. Abandoned factories, schools, cemeteries, theaters, and mansions are just some of the places you might bump into one—or more—ghosts.

I've researched old stories and new, hoping to create a book that will entertain, inform, and serve as a guide to some of the most haunted places in Milwaukee and southeastern Wisconsin.

Dead men (women, children, and pets) do tell tales. The proof is in the stories that follow.

Chapter 1

Ghosts 101

If you're like me, you probably don't know everything there is to know about ghosts. Whether there's a good chance you'll have a ghostly encounter, or just a slim one, I've listed a few things that are good to know. I've also thrown in some superstitions and a little trivia for good measure.

The definition most people associate with a ghost: disembodied soul. While "regular" people use the term *ghost* in connection with hauntings, parapsychologists usually use the term *apparition*.

Virtually all cultures believe (or believed at one time) that the ghosts of the dead are able to return to the world of the living. This includes the "walking dead" and "revenants."

Don't think ghosts stick around the world of the living for the fun of it. The majority of ghosts make themselves known for one of the following reasons: to comfort, to warn of imminent danger or death, or to impart important information.

Violent or sudden death may be one reason a ghost is tied to a particular place; some apparitions are earthbound spirits of the dead who are trapped among the living by business they were unable to finish when they were alive.

The term haunting refers to the recurring appearances of inexplicable phenomena, including hallucinations caused by a ghost or ghosts who are connected to a certain site. Some favorite "haunts" of the dead are former homes and locations where the dead actually died. Some ghosts haunt places they used to frequent when they were alive that may have held fond memories.

Is Your House Haunted?

So how do you know if your house is haunted? First, trust that "weird feeling" you have. It's trying really hard to tell you something is amiss.

If you have a shadow that moves across the room when the room is already dim and there's no light source to make a shadow, it could mean you have a ghost in the house.

Does the hair on the back of your neck or elsewhere stand on end when you're not in a draft? Are you depressed, experiencing a strong feeling that someone is watching you, tired all the time, hearing whispers or voices that have no source, wake up around three o'clock in the morning on a regular basis, feel chest pressure, loss of equilibrium, or paralyzed when you wake up—all with no medical explanation? Yup—a ghost might be involved.

Others' behavior might also give you a clue that a ghost is invading your space. If a small child talks to people he or she can't see (or the reverse), is fearful for no reason, or has an imaginary friend, you may have cause to believe his or her new "friend" is a ghost. (This happens more than you might imagine.) If a family member begins to have mood swings or acts like someone else with no medical explanation—you would do well to consider that a ghost is influencing their behavior.

Pets are a great way to tell if something otherworldly is inhabiting your world. Pets can come back from the dead like people, but living pets will act fearful and agitated if a ghost pet or animal is in the vicinity. Pets may also track things (like a ghost) we can't see.

Electrical problems might indicate a glitch with your wiring or power source, but they might also indicate a ghostly presence. Your clock also might stop ticking, your lights may turn off, or off and on, at will. Your thermostat may do a little self-adjusting. Your stereo and *TV* may suddenly act up, alone or in tandem, even if they're relatively new. And your computer and telephone? That's right; they're not immune to ghostly tinkering, either.

Remember the *Sixth Sense*? Cupboard doors opening when you leave the room could be a sign of an otherworldly presence. (Totally creepy.) A sudden drop or rise in temperature, or something in the air like perfume or cigarette smoke when there is no source are other indicators that your space may be haunted.

Strange mists or light, circular or irregular in shape, can signify the presence of a ghost. If you look at a photo and see black and white blobs that defy explanation, this also tells you that you may be seeing evidence of a spirit.

Ghosts themselves (if seen) can be transparent or semi-transparent, misty, or foggy. That sheet-covered stereotype you see in old *TV* shows could be a ghost, too. Many people have witnessed objects moving or levitating when a ghost is nearby.

If a ghost starts haunting you that was friendly to you in life, you might get a chilly feeling when he or she tries to make contact, but you won't have the sensation that you are in danger. You may even feel comforted—unless the ghost is trying to warn you of danger. In that case, the apprehension you feel will pass once you take action.

Which brings me to the crisis apparition. This kind of ghostly interaction can occur in dreams and also in waking visions. This type of contact is usually communication between the living and a person who is about to die, or has just expired.

If you hear your name called by a stranger, whatever you do, do not approach them because they could be a calling ghost in disguise. Calling ghosts are dangerous because they call out the names of those living so they take notice of them, only to lure the living to their death. Calling ghosts are best known in Hawaii, where disembodied female voices call out to you. Turn around and you'll make yourself vulnerable to sickness or death. At least that's the story.

Playing Keep Away With Ghosts!

Crossing oneself is probably one of the most familiar ways to ward off a ghost. Wearing or carrying chalcedony or obsidian will also keep a ghost away. Some of us may be familiar with carrying salt in a pocket or tossing it across a threshold to keep ghosts, witches, and evil spirits at arm's length.

Want to keep a ghost from rising from the dead? Simple. Just place an iron rod on a grave to prevent it from doing so. Warning: this is not for the weak of heart, or the just plain weak.

Horseshoes is more than a fun game. Hang a horseshoe over your doorway. It's a surefire way to keep a ghost from entering whatever abode you're trying to protect.

Silver jewelry, especially amulets, are said to keep ghosts and evil at bay. Many ghost researchers wear crucifixes, but any other religious symbol, as long as the wearer believes in its protective powers, is just as effective.

The expression "Don't speak ill of the dead" goes back to the idea that a ghost can come back to haunt you. If you are going to talk about someone who has passed, you might want to add "God rest his (or her) soul" somewhere in your commentary. It can't hurt.

Want to keep a ghost out of your house? Chalk a circle on your doors or doorstep, and ghosts can't enter. When drawing the circle, you must make sure the line is unbroken and joined completely.

Have a ghost you want to get rid of? Slam a door several times in a row. This is said to catch a ghost between the door and frame, forcing it to leave.

Orbs are another indicator that ghosts are, or were, in the area. Orbs are energy anomalies documented at sites believed to be haunted. You can't see orbs with the naked eye, but you can see them through infrared monitors or captured on photographic film.

Ghosts can also be captured on film as themselves or in less solid forms of themselves.

Ever wonder where the term *grateful dead* came from? This is from legends where the ghosts of the dead come back to the world of the living to grant gifts to people who are deserving of them. How cool is that?

Now let's visit some haunted sites and ghosts of Milwaukee.

Chapter 2

Twice Haunted

Creepy then. Creepy now.

This ghostly story can be divided into two hauntingly different parts. The first part is about a man who murdered his entire family and then shot himself in their apartment. The second part is about turning the same apartment building into a haunted house after being unable to successfully renovate it because of its ghostly occupants.

The story begins with an ordinary family who lived in an old apartment building, like many other families in Milwaukee, in the 1940s. This particular building was called the Cathedral Mayer-Krom Building. It was built in the late nineteenth century and was home to a retail store on the main floor. Part of the upper floor was devoted to small rooms; people came here for affordable medical and dental care. The rest of the rooms in the upper part of the building were used as apartments.

What makes this story so amazing is the fact that the Miltons, who lived in one of the upstairs apartments, were so un-amazing: They kept to themselves and stayed in their apartment most of the time. Like I said—pretty un-amazing stuff, especially for a big family living in close quarters.

No one can be sure, but those close quarters may have been a contributing factor to the tragedy that took place one fateful autumn day.

On October 3, 1943, the Milton family reportedly ceased to exist in human form. Around 3:00 p.m., Mr. Milton came home. He was unhappy; he'd been fired. He was also intoxicated.

First he argued with his wife. Then his children came home. It was then that events took a really ugly turn.

Mr. Milton grabbed a gun—loaded—and began threatening his family. Did his family react in terror? Did they think Mr. Milton was just letting off steam? The only thing we know for sure are the grisly events that followed.

Mr. Milton accidentally fired the shotgun. The bullet found its mark in one of his children. What follows defies belief. Mr. Milton, horrified no doubt, decided to cover his mistake...by shooting and killing his wife and the rest of his children. He then turned the gun on himself and pulled the trigger. That was the end of Mr. Milton, too.

This is where part two of the story begins. The upstairs apartment on Mitchell Street where the Miltons had once lived was now devoid of human life, but it was neither silent nor still. Strange things began happening upstairs. Objects from the offices began finding their way into the vacant apartment without the help of human hands. Pictures on the walls never stayed straight. Invisible interior un-decorators?

If there was a logical explanation, no one could put a name to it. An apparition specialist came to the building to find out if there was more in the apartment than met the eye. Surprise (not really)! A ghostly presence was discovered. It's also not surprising to learn that, soon after, all the living occupants of the apartment building vamoosed. Who wants to hang around a building where ghosts are still lurking about?

This is where part two of the story begins in earnest. Mars Distributing Incorporated bought the building in September, 1983, and moved in.

Mars found hallways in the middle of nowhere, rooms that were nailed shut, and windows that opened to blank walls. Huh? Mars knew they had to fix the problems; new tenants would never move·into a mess like this. Attempts to put things right were met with destruction. Experienced workers began getting injured. Progress was slow, too slow. Mars abandoned *Plan A* and went to *Plan B*— they would use the space for storage. Didn't happen, though.

Mars, innovators that they are, took into consideration the sensational history of the building and went to *Plan C*. They turned the mansion into a haunted house; construction was completed in September, 1993.

Visitors to the site of the multiple homicide report odd sensations, including chills. Some see dark shadows that move along with them, as if to keep tabs on them. Visitors I spoke with said the hair on their arms and neck stood on end the entire time they were inside the mansion—and they'd visited many haunted houses.

Is the Milton family still roaming the upstairs of the house? Would it surprise you?

The Mars Haunted House is located at 734 W. Historic Mitchell Street, and is open during the Halloween season. Visit them on the Web: www.marshauntedhouse.com. But better yet, visit the haunted house in person for a ghostly experience you will never forget.

Chapter 3

Van Buren Ghosts

Diane Guell and Jim Aho's lease didn't mention anything about ghosts, but they got them anyway.

When they began moving into the top floor apartment of their very old apartment building on Van Buren, the first ghost made its presence known almost immediately. This grandmotherly ghost seemed to watch over Diane as she settled in, making sure she was all right. The kindly presence didn't frighten Diane. Quite the opposite, she felt protected.

Diane wonders about the grandmotherly ghost. Had the old woman been a caretaker of some kind, a frequent visitor of the old building?

The ghost radiated a peaceful familiar feeling, which could mean she had a strong connection to the apartment building. This raised more questions. Had the apartment building been a hotel or dormitory? A school or clinic?

Diane soon had other things to think about when another ghost bullied his way into her life. The second ghost resides in the basement and is the kind of spirit most people go out of their way to avoid. Diane knows immediately when the mean ghost is around. She has the feeling of being watched. "You sense he's very bully-ish. He arouses every fear you ever had," she says of the basement ghost.

The feeling Diane gets when the bully ghost is near is akin to watching a horror film. It's that intense. Jim now goes downstairs to do the laundry so Diane doesn't have to subject herself to the bad vibes it gives off.

Jim was doing laundry in the basement at 6:30 a.m. one day when something caught his eye. He found a die, which was strange in itself. What really caught him off guard was the markings on the die.

At first, the die appeared to have the normal numbers: one, two, four and five, but in the positions where the three and six should be, there are images of ghosts instead. While the die doesn't look threatening, it definitely falls under the category of strange. Is the ghost die a peace offering from the mean ghost? Or is the die a remnant from a game of dice where someone used to conjure up the ghosts of the apartment building?

Diane is much more aware of things that don't fall under the category of normal, while Jim admits he isn't that in tune with ghostly presences. If something doesn't affect him directly, he usually just tunes it out. Luckily, the bully ghost keeps to himself most of the time, and that's just fine with Diane.

The grandmother and bully ghost might not be the only ghosts that share the building with Jim and Diane. Creaking and footsteps are often heard though no one is around, and the building itself could not be responsible for such sounds.

Diane recalls an unnerving experience that happened a short while ago. She still can't explain it. She and Jim were in their kitchen cooking when they saw a bright flash of light just above the level of Jim's head. Jim might have written it off, but Diane gave him what he calls a strange look and asked, "Wow! What was that?"

He knew immediately what she was talking about. At first, they thought it might be a reflection from someone's windshield. Then they looked in the direction of the window and realized the light couldn't have come from outside the building. The flash of light that appeared above Jim's head was directly in front of a dull non-reflective cupboard door; a reflection from a vehicle windshield would have been dull—not as bright as a flashbulb flash.

Diane takes it all in stride. The grandmotherly ghost doesn't bother her, and she avoids the nasty one whenever possible. Someday, she plans to do a historical search of the building's background to shed light on the otherworldly tenants.

Ghost dice; two angles.
Courtesy of Jim Aho.

Chapter 4

Lady Elgin's Ghosts

Emmett Jordan of Milwaukee, a charter member of Discovery World/Pier Wisconsin, knows more about the tragic shipwreck of the *Lady Elgin* than most, thanks to countless hours of meticulous research. His ancestors, rum and medicine importer Nick McGrath, and Milwaukee US Harbormaster Martin Dooley (aka, Doorley), were victims of the historic sinking of the steamer *USM Lady Elgin* by the schooner *Augusta* of Oswego. The tragedy claimed the lives of 300 aboard the *Elgin* that fateful night.

The *Lady Elgin* left Chicago on September 7, 1860, an hour or two before midnight, carrying about 400 passengers, many of whom were returning to Milwaukee. Captain Jack Wilson, a veteran lakes captain, was in charge of the vessel.

Three hundred excursionists were on board, including many members of Milwaukee's militia and fire companies. Represented were the Union Guards, Light Guards, Green Jagers, Black Jagers, Rifles, Milwaukee City Band, Jager Old Time Fiddlers, and the Shakespeare Club. Fifty ordinary passengers and a crew of thirty-five officers and men rounded out the rest of those on board.

A storm fueled by moderately high winds was already pounding Chicago when the *Lady Elgin* left shore. In the early morning hours of September 8, a particularly violent squall of rain and wind hit the steamer and the schooner. When the collision occurred, the Lady Elgin was approximately ten miles from shore, off Winetka, about sixteen north of Chicago.

Some accounts say the *Augusta*, with Captain Darius Malott in charge, was sailing west by south. Others believe the *Augusta* was sailing east by south when she hit the *Elgin*. If the *Augusta* had been sailing eastward, shipping laws of the time would have had her turning south to avoid collision. Making matters even more confusing: A recently enacted clause of law gave schooners the right of way because some steamers were running down schooners and fishing vessels, even when they were at anchor. Whether the *Augusta* was in the right or wrong, all agree she struck the *Elgin's* port side.

At the time of impact, most of the passengers had not retired for the evening, in part because few had cabins. The steamer was chiefly a freighter with a large salon/saloon like many floating gambling casinos. That night, the forward cabin served as a dance hall, though many passengers were seasick. Moments after the Augusta crashed into the Elgin in the wee hours of September 8, 1860, all was still.

Captain Wilson immediately ordered a lifeboat to be lowered to discover the extent of the damage, but the *Elgin* began to fill rapidly with water. Adding to the confusion, many of the crew used the few small lifeboats near the pilot house to flee the ship. Only Captain Wilson, of the ship's officers, is recognized as having stayed on board to organize rescue attempts. The damaged vessel then turned to steam toward shore after the collision, her wreckage floating southwest-ward.

It's likely US Harbormaster Martin Dooley and many of the Union Guards died when they obeyed orders to go down to the cargo hold to launch passenger yawls, throw cattle overboard, and try to shift the cargo. The decks most likely collapsed on top of them when the ship rapidly began breaking into pieces.

The regular crew, and probably Dooley because he was a steam engineer himself (along with a number of the Guards), were able to prevent a boiler explosion by tending to safety valves before the decks collapsed.

By then, however, many of the *Elgin's* crew had already abandoned the wreckage, hampering second class life plank distribution from locked storage closets.

It's not difficult to imagine the terror and panic of those aboard the sinking ship as the wind and rain assaulted them. The waters of Lake Michigan, more than 300 feet deep, awaited them below. Around the ship, waves crashed together, breaking and destroying whatever met between them as lightning lit the black sky.

The cause of the wreck is murky to this day. Was the crash an accident? Was it a deliberate act? Emmett's unconfirmed theory is that an accountant owner of the *Elgin*, eager to maximize the number of round trips to Lake Superior before the Soo locks froze, might have insisted Captain Wilson leave the Chicago port despite the stormy weather.

It was also rumored the *Lady Elgin* was about to be sold to a Milwaukee firm. Any of these reasons would have warranted getting *Lady Elgin* on her way back to Milwaukee without delay.

The Chicago tug, the McQueen, had to wait out the storm before attempting rescue. When the tug finally reached the wreck, the crew found a huge bow section anchored and floating near the sunken engine and boiler section.

Was Malott lying about his sailing direction and his claim of having a mast lantern lit when the *Augusta* struck the *Elgin*? The Polytechnic Association of the American Institute testified that the type of oil lantern that would have been aboard the schooner that night would have blown out on a windy rainy night such as the night of the crash.

This substantiates a number of accounts that the vessel was unlit. Cautious schooners rode out the storm with sails down, so perhaps this was a deliberate ramming attack by the *Augusta*, a common maneuver in the 1812 and Civil Wars. Captain Wilson perished, so it will never be known if the anchor of the *Elgin* was lowered, or the *Elgin* was in fact steaming toward shore.

While researching the shipwreck, Emmett discovered one of the last tasks Martin Dooley performed was the publishing of the latest manifest of scheduled ship arrivals and departures; Dooley would not be among the arrivals.

The ship's clerk fled the wreckage without his passenger roster. This made it almost impossible to confirm the identities of the lost. Adding to the confusion: while clerks working at Dooley, Martin, Dousman & Company steamboat dock in Milwaukee recorded the two hundred Milwaukeeans who boarded after the *Lady Elgin* arrived in Milwaukee, twelve hours late due to a storm up north, they didn't record the at least one hundred others who went home after warnings of dangerous fog.

The story does not end here, though a new chapter does begin. Ghostly music from the dead musicians on board the sunken *Lady Elgin* echoed through the *Augusta's* holds on later voyages. It was reported that ghosts even tried to set fire to the *Augusta*, which was renamed the *Colonel Cook* and sent to the Atlantic for a while.

Nick McGrath, who lived on Erie Street in the Third Ward, floated into the mouth of the Milwaukee River and went ashore at Dooley Martin, Dousman & Company, Forwarding and Commission Agents, at South Pier, foot of Erie Street...one month after the wreck of the *Lady Elgin*.

Some say they have seen ghostly figures struggling toward the Lake Michigan shore. Are they victims of the *Lady Elgin* who floated to shore for days after the wreck, still struggling to return home to their loved ones?

Captain Wilson is remembered for his heroic efforts in this Lake Michigan tragedy, but others like Emmett Jordan's ancestors also played a very important part in trying to save the ship from even greater disaster.

A Wisconsin Historical Marker stands on North Water and East Erie Streets to commemorate the sinking of the *Lady Elgin*.

Emmett Jordan, in addition to his passion for history, is an electronic engineer, past member of the Wisconsin Marine Historical Society, Milwaukee County Genealogical Society, and Fellow of the Royal Society of Antiquaries of Ireland.

Chapter 5
Pfister Hotel

Mr. Charles Pfister died in 1927, but if you visit the Pfister Hotel located at 424 East Wisconsin Avenue, in downtown Milwaukee, you just might see him anyway.

Pfister and his sister, Louise, built the premiere hotel in 1893. The building is incredible by anyone's standards. One of its most eye-catching features is the stunningly beautiful three-story lobby, flanked by a huge marble staircase on one end and a massive fireplace on the other end.

The Pfister Hotel, Milwaukee.

Charles was an art collector who accumulated many Victorian paintings, including numerous paintings of dogs, which still grace the walls of the hotel today.

Mr. Pfister has been seen in a number of various locations in the hotel. He's been spotted walking down an eighth floor hallway with his dog, taking a ride in an elevator, looking over the lobby from a spot on the grand staircase, and standing in the gallery above the ballroom. The people who see him immediately recognize the distinguished-looking gentleman from his portrait.

Others haven't seen Mr. Pfister, but have reported seeing ghostly dogs in the hotel hallways.

Adrian Beltre, a former Los Angeles Dodgers' third baseman, once stayed at the Pfister Hotel. His experience there unnerved him so much that he even told Sports Illustrated about it.

Beltre says he heard knocking in the hallway and on his door, and then heard more of the same coming from behind his head-board. In addition, the *TV* and air conditioning in his room kept turning off. Beltre complained he only got two hours of sleep in three nights.

If "Charlie" Pfister was trying to improve the odds the Brewers would win against the Dodgers, his efforts failed. The Dodgers won two out of three games of that series.

People have differing theories about why Pfister makes so many appearances. Some believe he is making comparisons between where he is now and his grand hotel. And others believe Pfister is merely checking to make sure that his hotel is still offering the same personal-touch services it offered when he was alive.

Pfister can rest easy. The Pfister Hotel is still known as the "Jewel of Milwaukee," offering world-class amenities; Condé Nast Traveler once named the Pfister Hotel among the world's best places to stay.

So the next time you visit or stay at the Pfister, don't be surprised if Charlie crosses your path. But don't worry. He's just making the rounds.

Chapter 6

Grumpy Joe

Twenty-Seventh Street is the longest street in Milwaukee. It's also the address of one very grumpy ghost.

The occupants of the charming two-story home where the ghost resides call him Grumpy Joe; that's what the kids in the neighborhood called him when he was alive.

Joe is believed to be the third owner of the home. A former neighbor who lived down the street remembers Joe as being a crabby old man who was always looking for trouble. This assessment might be based on the fact that he was a young boy when he knew Joe, and also because he personally inspired Grumpy Joe's wrath when he hit a baseball through the old man's window, not once but twice.

The former neighbor recalls at least four baseballs going through Joe's window one particular summer when he was twelve or thirteen. It seemed like no matter where the neighborhood kids played ball, they would invariably end up smacking a baseball through Joe's upstairs window. It was like the glass had a bull's eye on it.

If you were to ask the neighborhood kids in those days to name one thing about Joe, they would name two: One—he was always looking through one of his ultra clean windows, and two—he always had a scowl on his face.

As Grumpy Joe's two daughters got older and eventually began dating, he would watch them leave with their dates, first from a first floor window, then from a second floor window when he could no longer see them from the first.

Up the stairs and down, up the stairs and down. Grumpy Joe's daughters would just hug him and roll their eyes at his over-protectiveness.

When Grumpy Joe's wife died, his trips up and down the stairs became almost nonstop. He kept watch for her for years.

Then Joe's daughters moved away. He got even grumpier and made even more trips up and down the stairs. He spent more time walking up and down the steps in his home than most people did going about their daily chores.

The relentless trips up and down the stairs weren't necessarily a waste of time. More than once he alerted the police to a break-in or burglary in the immediate neighborhood.

When Joe died, the house was sold to an elderly couple. The couple complained about the ever-creaking stairs, but they were oblivious to the fact they were sharing their home with a ghost.

It wasn't until the elderly couple died and the current residents, Tom and Deana, moved in that they knew exactly what the relentless creaking of the steps meant.

Tom lived at the end of the block when he was a kid; he was yet another boy who had belted a baseball through one of Grumpy Joe's windows one summer.

The hardwood staircase Grumpy Joe uses is a conversation piece. You can literally see the steps sag along with a noticeable creak as he either goes upstairs or downstairs. This might be disconcerting to some, but Joe never goes anywhere else in the house. Tom and Deana are careful not to interrupt Joe's trips up or down. After all, Joe pretty much leaves them alone.

When Tom and Deana had a little boy a year after they moved in, they were understandably concerned. As baby Cody got older, Tom and Deana worried he might get in Grumpy Joe's way.

Cody began to crawl; they monitored his every move up and down the stairs. Cody began to walk; they made sure he toddled up the stairs when Joe was elsewhere.

One day, Cody slipped away from Deana's watchful eye. By the time she found him, he was already halfway up the stairs. As she rushed to make sure he didn't fall, she heard the unmistakable sound of Grumpy Joe coming down the stairs. Not wanting to scare Cody, she came to a complete stop and held her breath.

Deana saw the steps above Cody sag slightly and heard the accompanying creak as Joe began walking down the stairs. Then, as Cody grabbed the railing above him and took a step up, the creaking stopped. This was a first. Once Grumpy Joe decided to go up or down, he did so without stopping or changing directions. Cody took a step up. Grumpy Joe took a step up, then Cody, then Joe, Cody, then Joe—until Cody toddled off to his upstairs room.

Then the stairs began creaking again as Grumpy Joe finished his trip down the stairs.

Did the kids in the neighborhood peg Grumpy Joe wrong? Maybe they did, maybe they didn't. The current owners, however, are happy to have Grumpy Joe in their home, keeping a watchful eye on their young son.

Chapter 7

St. James Episcopal Church

S t. James Episcopal Church, probably the oldest stone church in Milwaukee, is located at 833 West Wisconsin Avenue, on Milwaukee's West Side. It has architectural significance because of its age, as well as being one of the finest examples known of a stone Gothic Revival Church.

St. James has been listed in the National Register of Historic Places since 1979, and was designated a Milwaukee Landmark in 1980. It is the home of the oldest Episcopal congregation on the West Side and at least two ghosts.

One of the things that makes this church interesting is that it was once a stop on the Underground Railroad. What makes this church unique and not just a little fascinating, is the fact that it still houses bits and pieces of a cemetery that was supposedly moved long ago.

When the land at the site was donated to the church, its graves were moved to Cavalry Cemetery. But not all of them. Among the bones and grave markers that still reside at 833 West Wisconsin Avenue are a tombstone belonging to Lydia Vinton and a marker for Dr. John Parmele. Lydia was twenty-eight when she died in 1839. Dr. Parmele was forty-three when he died in 1844.

Could Lydia or Dr. Parmele be responsible for the strange happenings at the church? When asked, some members of the church say they believe ghosts do inhabit the basement; others politely change the subject.

One thing everyone agrees upon: The basement is creepy enough to be labeled haunted. There's a doorway in the basement that leads to a secret staircase, which in turn leads to the altar. The basement floor of the church is dirt, and city steam pipes above your head fill the air with an unpleasant musty odor. And then there's that "feeling" you get when you're down there. It's as if someone's keeping an eye on you.

Things go missing inside the church; strange sounds have been heard by many. Recently, the lights went off and a door closed for no reason. When nearby church workers were questioned, no one admitted to turning off the lights or shutting the door.

Lydia? Dr. Parmele? Or is it the ghost of someone else beneath the dirt basement floor waiting to be discovered? Some members of St. James go out of their way to make sure they're not in the basement, just in case.

Chapter 8

Dousman Dunkel Behling Inn

O ver the years, countless reports of paranormal activity on the premises have given this inn its haunting reputation.

The Elmbrook Historical Society presently occupies this historically preserved stage coach inn built in the 1840s and maintains it as a museum. It's located at 1075 Pilgrim Parkway in the town of Brookfield, but once stood at the corner of Bluemound and Watertown Plank Roads, the original route of horse drawn carriages along the Watertown Plank Road. This route was heavily traveled during the time it was used as an inn.

This long-named inn can be found halfway between Milwaukee and Waukesha. It was open for business during the period surrounding the Civil War, between 1857 and 1872. Like most other commercial ventures featuring the stagecoach, it was put out of business when the railroads came to town at the end of the nineteenth century.

Depending on which account you read, the inn was either built by Talbot Dousman, whose brother, Hercules, later built the Villa Louis in Prairie du Chien, or Michael Dousman, a fur trader and entrepreneur from Michigan.

The short list of ownership includes Daniel Brown, a Connecticut Yankee, who operated it from 1857 to 1872. Frederick Zimdars, a farmer, bought the inn in 1873. From 1887 to 1977, Charles Dunkel and his descendants owned the inn. Finally, the Elmbrook Historical Society took over ownership when John Behling, a grandson of Charles Dunkel, presented it to them. The inn was then moved to its present site, which was once owned by the first Surgeon General of Wisconsin, Dr. Erastus B. Wolcott. Whew! Not so short after all.

The most famous spirit said to haunt the property is a dark ghostly figure said to wander the upstairs when no one is in the building. This same figure is said to rush visitors—men or women, it's not sexist—with such force they fly backwards off the porch. Subtlety apparently isn't its strong suit.

If you stand near the guest house or blacksmith shop, you might experience negative feelings so powerful you can become physically ill. Parts of the buildings themselves add to the strangeness of the site; doors reportedly slam when no one is present, and window panes flutters as if someone is noiselessly pounding on them.

The inn has been completely restored, and is furnished with authentic Wisconsin antiques. This may be one reason the ghosts of the inn feel so at home here. Some visitors to the inn have seen a well-dressed man smoking a pipe just inside the doorway, and have smelled tobacco. This same man disappears into the wall when you walk toward him.

If you're interested in spotting a different sort of ghost, take in the smoke house, ice house, smithy shop, and original 1862 Woodside School Bell Tower. Visitors to these buildings have reported seeing small shadows flitting here and there. Former students?

If you're lucky, or perhaps unlucky, you may come face to face with the pushy dark figure said to haunt the inn.

Chapter 9

The House On 15th Avenue

This house is really haunted; two members of Milwaukee Madness 2U sent me stories about their experiences there.

The first to share her story is Ardith Ann Richter. She and her first husband, Dean, bought their South Milwaukee home on 15th Avenue in 1994. They had no idea ghosts were already in residence.

Ivan, Barry, and Melanie grew up there, as well as several other young people who lived with Ardith and the kids from 1986 to 1994.

During that time, a little girl who died in a fire in the house in the early 1900s, became a frequent visitor. The little girl ghost, in her best dress, would whisper to those in the house. Sometimes she would pet the cat, have a comic read to her...or have some fresh bread and jam—just like any living girl might do.

Ardith remembers one lazy fall Sunday afternoon when her second husband, Ed, was sitting in the living room reading the paper. A small voice next to his elbow whispered to him, "Read the comics, please!"

Not thinking anything of it, Ed read the comics for a minute without looking up to see who had made the request. Then, finally noticing he was the only one in the living room, he went to the kitchen and told Ardith, "I just read to no one!"

Ardith laughed at his shocked expression and said, "Not really. She just likes to have the comics read out loud. I think they make more sense to her that way."

The little girl ghost also liked jam. Ardith used to leave fresh bread and jam on the table just for her. One Sunday dinner when she and her husband were setting the table, Ardith set out a plate with a spoonful of fresh pear jam and a piece of bread at the end of the table. By the time their meal was finished, the plate with jam and bread was no longer as Ardith had left it.

Ed could never understand why Ardith did this, but the plate of jam and bread she left out for the little girl ghost was always disturbed by the end of the meal.

The little girl ghost was not the only ghost that visited the 15th Avenue house. An older lady ghost and a nasty older man ghost, who once lived at the house before they died, often made their presences known.

Apparently, the old couple liked the house too much to move on.

Rebecca, another Milwaukee Madness 2U member, tells her story about the house. "I became a believer (in ghosts)," she says. Until she lived there, she always thought of ghosts as just nice spooky stories without a whole lot of reality behind them. She soon found the house to be "freaky" with paranormal activity, causing her to change her mind forever about ghosts.

When Rebecca initially moved into the house, things began happening—strange things she couldn't explain. At one point, she thought her cousins were trying to scare her, but later found out they weren't—the ghosts in the house were responsible.

Rebecca lived with the ghostly activity (the ghosts hadn't actually hurt her) until the house was sold. Not long after, she ran into one of the former owners. After telling him about some of the incidents that happened to her while she lived there, he said he had the same experiences himself while living in the house.

It's safe to say the new residents of the house on 15th Avenue have had a ghostly experience or two themselves.

Chapter 10

Forest Home Cemetery

Forest Home Cemetery is so haunted it's even mentioned in a list of most haunted cemeteries in Haunted America Tours web site. The cemetery hasn't made the top ten list yet, but as far as many visitors are concerned, it should be number one.

This isn't some backwoods cemetery; it's as beautiful as a park (if you pretend the headstones don't exist). Its rolling grounds are accented by a pond and concrete bridge. That's probably one of the reasons some of Milwaukee's wealthiest and famous, including beer barons and war heroes, are spending eternity here.

If you're looking for unusual headstones (how about a concrete boat topper?), you've come to the right place. If you're looking for beautiful marble monuments, this is also the place to see them. Looking for ghosts? Forest Home has a plethora of unearthly spirits in residence.

You might encounter a ghost on the hill next to the pond on the north side of the cemetery. People that stand close to the pool sometimes report feeling sick to their stomach. Some get instant, horrific headaches.

There have been numerous reports of people having visions here, too. Of those that do, most see coffins or the dead. One man I spoke to said he saw a coffin containing a man who bolted upright into a sitting position. The man in the coffin turned and looked straight at him. Yikes! Needless to say the visitor left the cemetery as fast as he could.

Go ahead, take a picture inside the cemetery. Many report capturing orbs—that is, if your camera doesn't go dead on you. Shadowy figures behind the main subject of your photo are often reported, as well as washed out and bright areas that can't be explained.

The first burial in the cemetery was Orville Cadwell, on August 5, 1850. Many others were soon buried in the cemetery because of an outbreak of cholera.

One possible explanation for the ever-present feeling of being watched is the fact the cemetery was built on top of Paleo Indian burial mounds. The land that houses the cemetery also intersects a particularly large number of effigy mounds.

Over sixty of these earthworks were catalogued by Increase Lapham, a famous pioneer scientist who also happens to be buried at Forest Home. One of the earthworks was a rare intaglio of a panther. Unfortunately, none of the earthworks remain today.

Some notable people buried at Forest Home include: Billy Mitchell, "father" of the U.S. Air Force, William Davidson, co-founder of the Harley-Davidson Motorcycle Company, Sherburn Becker, "boy mayor" of Milwaukee, Sherman Booth, abolitionist and newspaper editor, Alfred Lunt and Lynn Fontanne, a famous Broadway acting team, and Christopher Sholes, inventor of the modern typewriter.

Famous beer barons (hey, that's what Milwaukee's famous for) buried in Forest Home include August Krug, founder of what eventually became the Joseph Schlitz Brewing Company and Frederick Pabst of Pabst Brewing Company. A cenotaph for Joseph Schlitz, who perished in a shipwreck in 1875 off the coast of England, also exists in the cemetery.

Another monument, the Newhall House Monument, is a mass grave for sixty-four people who died in the Newhall House Fire of 1883. Seventy-one people died in the fire; forty-three were never identified.

Is it any wonder some experience gut-wrenching pain when they visit this incredibly haunted cemetery?

Chapter 11

Witch Ghost

If you drive down the curving road along the lake shore of Fox Point, you can't help but notice the beautiful homes and breathtaking views.

But one home, hidden behind a chain-link fence topped with barbed wire and dozens of garish statues in the yard, seems as out of place here as an elephant emerging from nearby Lake Michigan.

Mary Nohl, a talented artist, once lived in this house in what is otherwise a serene, partially secluded area. The out-of-this-world house and strange grounds can't help but capture your imagination. So do the rumors that surround her life. People still talk about the tragic deaths of Mary's husband and young son, who drowned in a boating accident. They perished before her very eyes.

This is when supposition comes into play. Some say Mary began making warding statues to keep the spirits of the water away, so they wouldn't take her life as well. A different story, no doubt crafted by the teenagers in the area, claims Mary killed her husband and son and hid them among her statues at her home, called the "Witch's House" by many.

The true story of the Fox Point witch is much less thrilling. Mary was born in 1914 and graduated from the Art Institute of Chicago in the late 1930s. She came to the cottage in Fox Point in the 1960s and began sculpting in earnest. Many of her creations are made of concrete and things that washed ashore. Her statues, because they are not classically beautiful, are considered by some to be ugly, even satanic in nature. She was also an accomplished painter, wood carver, and jewelry designer—not what you would call typical "witch" activities. Those who were fortunate enough to know her when she was alive say she was a good friend and caring person. Adding to the mystery surrounding the talented artist: she never remarried.

For years, people have come from miles around to see her work and her home—most of them teenagers. Ms. Nohl took this twisted interest in her work in stride. The kind-hearted woman never prosecuted trespassers.

She died in 2001, donating her cottage and millions of dollars to the Kohler Foundation and the Greater Milwaukee Foundation. She believed there was no better life than the life of an artist.

The Kohler Foundation has expressed a desire to open the cottage as a museum, but Mary's Fox Point neighbors are tired of decades of constant drive-bys. They aren't eager to embrace a new wave of visitors, even if they might be visiting for a different reason.

In 2005, the Wisconsin Preservation Trust listed the Mary Nohl site as one of the ten most endangered properties in Wisconsin. It's also been nominated as a Milwaukee County Landmark.

Many ghost hunters say they've seen shadows pass between the concrete people and animals behind the fence. They swear they've see Mary's face pressed close to the dark grated windows looking back at them. Others say they feel a strong, almost physical presence when they stop. And there are others who swear they've seen Mary herself walking among her strangely beautiful creations.

Ghost—maybe. Witch—never. Misunderstood by many—yes.

Chapter 12

North Side Ghosts

The hair on the back of your neck stands on end for no reason. You hear a thin pleading voice...or maybe a scream, but there's no one there.

If you're on the North Side of Milwaukee, especially the 2300 block of Eighth and the Ember Lane Bridge, and you feel a sense of unease, it just might be the ghostly presence of a murder victim. Two strings of vicious murders took place near there, claiming the lives of more than a dozen people.

The first sequence of murders in this "high-crime area" took place from 1979-1980 in a neighborhood in the middle of Eighth, Holton, Center, and Garfield Streets. At the time when the murders were being committed, most of them didn't get more than a brief mention in the newspapers—they apparently didn't seem out of the ordinary for a city of Milwaukee's size. At first glance, the murders seemed to have no common bond. The victims were men and women, black and white; some were stabbed to death while others were bludgeoned.

Detective Roosevelt Harrell, however, suspected the murders were linked. Unfortunately, it wasn't until a number of murders had occurred that he was able to take on the case.

The first murder involved Della Mae Liggins, 69, a retired school teacher who lived on N. Eighth Street. On July 19, 1979, she was stabbed to death. Missing: her 1972 Pontiac. A ghostly woman has been seen in what is believed to be her backyard. She was a good friend to many.

On August 10th, Florence Burkard, 78, N. Hubbard Street, was stabbed 43 times—to death. She had been dying of cancer at the time of the vicious attack. Her purse was left behind on the kitchen table.

Helen Wronski, 79, the next to die, was beaten to death. She lived on N. Holton Street.

Incredibly, the next attack didn't make the paper until the victim died several months later. Charles Golston, 63, who resided on N. Buffam Street was attacked with a claw hammer. The attack took place on January 25, 1980. He spent the rest of his life in a coma, until early May, when he finally passed away.

Bernard Fonder, 49, who lived on N. Booth Street, died of multiple blows to the head. He apparently had a premonition of dying, because he gave his neighbor a note with the name and address of his former roommate. He told his neighbor to call the police if anything should happen to him; his roommate had beaten him on a previous occasion.

When Mr. Fonder was found murdered, fingerprints were found; the roommate was questioned, and later arrested. The roommate, however, was released because the police didn't have the evidence they needed.

The attacks continued. If the good citizens of Milwaukee's North Side had known what real danger they were in, they might have begun locking their doors and taking more precautions. As it stood, public awareness was little to none.

Sandy Ellis was beaten and slashed on April 14, 1980, but miracle of miracles, she lived by pretending to be unconscious.

On April 25, Helen Bellamy, 30 years old and the mother of four, was murdered. Detective Harrell was finally able to get the okay to get a special investigative unit together. Helen Bellamy had been sexually assaulted and beaten with a tire iron until she died.

Harrell and Lieutenant Carl Ruscitti cracked the case. David Van Dyke was arrested and convicted of six counts of murder and one count of attempted murder. Van Dyke will be 103 years old before he is eligible for parole. Small consolation to the murder victims' loved ones, but at least there was a sense of closure. The loved ones of the next string of murders weren't so lucky.

A dozen black women were strangled to death on Milwaukee's North Side between the mid-1980s and mid-1990s. Some say they get an eerie feeling when they're near the North Avenue Dam and Ember Lane Bridge, where two of the women were murdered. A sort of inexplicable sadness envelops many, even if it's a sunny day.

The first to die during the serial killer's murderous spree was Debra L. Harris, 31. After her body was pulled from the Menomonee River, east of the Ember Lane Bridge on October 10, 1986, it was discovered that she had been tied up using a "clove hitch" type of knot. This murder was especially vicious because Debra had been beaten with a brick and strangled.

Nineteen-year-old Tanya Miller was another victim of the strangler's rampage. Her body was found on October 11, 1986, in the 2100 block of North Twenty-Eighth Street; a clove hitch had been used to tie her.

Ophelia Preston was strangled to death with a rope and dumped in a garbage cart in the 1700 block of King Drive in 1994. She had the phone number of city worker in her pocket. The worker was questioned but never charged. A "crying ghost woman" has been seen in a nearby alley, who vanishes when you approach.

Florence McCormick was strangled with a clothesline just one block away from where Maryetta Griffin, another victim, was found. Florence was only 28 years old when she was found on April 24, 1995, in a vacant house in the 600 block of Locust Street. A clove hitch was also used to tie her.

Sheila Farrior was the mother of five children and a member of the Friendship Club, a place that offered counseling to drug addicts. The 36-year-old was found strangled to death on June 27, 1995, in a vacant house in the 1400 block of West Chambers Street.

Rasheda Dickerson's strangled body was found on March 11, 1996, wrapped in a quilt near the North Avenue Dam. She was 17 years old. Her killer tied her using a clove hitch like several of the other murder victims.

On June 20, 1997, workers fixing up a vacant house in the 2900 block of North 5th Street found the body of Joyce Ann Mims. She was 41 years old, had no criminal record, and had, like the other women, been strangled.

Wanda Harris, 38, was beaten and strangled to death. Her body was found on November 9, 1997, beneath some old tires in the 2000 block of West Fond Du Lac Avenue.

Joyce Ann Mims knew George L. "Mule" Jones, who pleaded guilty to killing Shameika Carter, 24, one of the other victims. Jones denied killing Mims, despite a lie detector test that indicated he was lying. Jones was never charged with Joyce Ann's murder.

Maryetta Griffin left the world of the living on February 17, 1998. She was 39 years old and had been strangled to death by someone's bare hands. Maryetta's life was filled with violence and death. When she was 26, she was raped, her face and throat slashed, and left for dead; a drunk driver killed the father of her children; and when Maryetta was 13, her father was shot six times and killed.

William Avery was arrested for Maryetta's murder, but he never went to jail for it. He was, however, sentenced to 10 years in prison for running a drug house.

Yvonne Reynolds was murdered about three weeks before her body was discovered on September 1, 1995 in an apartment building in the 2600 block of North Richards Street. Yvonne died of manual strangulation.

The Milwaukee Police Department was accused of not giving these cases high priority because the victims were black. Most of the murders were never solved, despite the assistance of the FBI.

Is this perhaps one of the reasons so many restless souls haunt Milwaukee's North Side?

Chapter 13

DeKoven Center

The DeKoven Center, founded and chartered in 1852, is an Episcopal retreat and conference center located on twenty acres on the shores of Lake Michigan. Before it was the DeKoven Center, it served as a number of different things: Racine College, an Episcopal seminary, a boys' prep school, and a home for Anglican nuns.

Visitors to the center include Mary Todd Lincoln, who considered the school for her son, Tad. Others like Ralph Waldo Emerson lectured here, and General Billy Mitchell, called the father of the U.S. Air Force, was a graduate of the school.

There are many rumors surrounding the DeKoven Center. It is said to have been an orphanage once and that a suicide took place on campus, but the DeKoven Center was never an orphanage. It's also been said that James DeKoven, the headmaster of the school for many years, took his own life. Not true: He died of apoplexy at the college on March 22, 1879.

Rumors aside, numerous reports of a strange ghostly figure in the basement and hallways have been, and continue to be, reported.

Though others have undoubtedly died on the sprawling premises, no one has more reason to stick around than the Reverend Dr. James DeKoven himself. He was an educator, priest, and leader of the Anglo-Catholic movement in the Episcopal Church. He once taught at another haunted site featured in this book, the Nashotah House.

After DeKoven died, he was laid to rest on the grounds of what is now the DeKoven Center.

The DeKoven Center has a long and illustrious past, but not without controversy. DeKoven defended the use of incense, candles, and liturgical gestures like kneeling and bowing at the General Conventions of 1871 and 1874.

His position regarding the use of rituals was divisive; because of it, he wasn't able to get the required consents from the dioceses he needed to become a bishop.

We may never know if it is DeKoven's ghost or the ghost of someone else associated with the center that roams the grounds and buildings. Regardless, a little campus spirit never hurt anyone.

Chapter 14

La Belle Cemetery

This cemetery in Oconomowoc has a reputation for being haunted, and the more you dig, the more strange stories you unearth.

La Belle is a hilly cemetery set in a beautiful location that has many extraordinary markers. A number of those statues and crypts are of particular interest to those in search of a paranormal experience.

The cemetery is unique because it has a bridge that spans part of Fowler Lake as an entrance to the cemetery. (The other entrance is accessible through Lapham Street.) La Belle is also bordered to the west by Fowler Lake. Visitors say they experience a "twitchy" feeling when they drive over the bridge on their way into the cemetery, and are overcome by strong conflicting feelings of sadness, peace, and unease.

Most people, however, think of the statue of the young girl when they think of La Belle.

The creepiest story, one which many people have reported, is the one in which they see a young girl detaching herself from the statue and walking directly to the lake and drowning herself. Others swear the statue becomes a ghost and walks slowly to the lake. When you ask these people who the ghost is, they will invariably say she is one of the two women buried in the Nathusius plot, directly in front of the statue.

The statue is easy to find. It's been described as an angel; others say it is a girl holding what looks like Easter lilies. The statue stands next to a cross.

Members of the Nathusius family buried in front of the statue include: father Carl, mother Louise, brother Wilhelm, and daughter Carolina.

Fowler Lake is just a few yards away from the statue so the sightings of a young girl walking to the lake are not farfetched. Some of the resulting problems that have been blamed on witnessing the walk to the water do, however, seem a little farfetched: blindness and mysterious deaths.

While it is possible one of the deceased Nathusius females committed suicide by drowning, one thinks someone in the area would remember the event so as to put an end to speculation. One story has Mary (one name given to the statue) ending her human life by jumping off the bridge at the entrance of the cemetery. No one knows Mary's surname, or when the suicide supposedly took place.

This same statue, whose ghost is also known as the "anchor lady" statue because she's said to walk away from the Nathusius plot with an anchor tied around her leg. The ghost carries the anchor to the lake with her, lowers herself and "dies" of suffocation.

Some that take photos of the statue say her eyes always appear much blacker than when they are standing in front of the statue in person. They also say that when you stand directly in front of the statue, the air goes very cold.

Some have reported seeing blood drip from the statue, but when they touch it, it's dry. Some have put makeup on the statue's face (odd, yes) only to have it immediately disappear.

People who visit the grave, whether they are family members, friends, or those who are there to see the statue/ghost walk into the lake, often leave coins and other things in the statue's hands.

The girl statue isn't La Belle's only attraction. If you go into certain areas of the cemetery, like the small wooded area near the second entrance, you may experience trouble with your camera. This has been noted by paranormal investigators and amateur ghost hunters alike.

One couple I talked with said they were parked about a half block away from the girl statue and suddenly couldn't get either of their cameras to work, when they'd been working just five minutes earlier. In addition, when the couple returned to their locked car, the windshield wipers were on and the radio was playing at full volume. They said the experience was so unnerving that it was a year before they returned—only to have a similar experience.

Another time, a young man standing near the statue suddenly had his car turn on, engine rev, lights flash, and just as suddenly, shut off. His car keys were in his pocket and he was some distance from his car.

The girl statue is not the only statue said to have a ghost associated with it. There is also a crypt that moves on its own, and another that is said to open of its own volition.

A crypt with the surname Kohl, located in the center of the cemetery, gives people a feeling so strange it cannot be put into words.

Chances are good, you'll see or "feel" at least one ghost if you pay a visit to La Belle.

Strang monument.

Chapter 15

Wisconsin King

James Jesse Strang was born Jesse James Strang on March 21, 1813, in New York. When he was twelve years old, he was baptized as a Baptist. On February 24, 1844, he was baptized as a member of the Church of Jesus Christ of Latter Day Saints in Nauvoo, Illinois.

The latter event, no pun intended, marks the beginning of what would be a very extraordinary life—even if it ended violently and prematurely. Copper-haired James Strang was the first and only man to be crowned king in the United States. (He switched his first and second names around because he thought King James sounded more regal than King Jesse.)

Even as a child, he had big dreams for himself, despite the fact he was possessed of delicate health. Differing reports say Strang was both intellectually gifted and mentally retarded.

When James was twenty-three, he was admitted to the New York Bar. He married Mary Perce the same year. As fate would have it, Mary's sister was married to Moses Smith, a founder of the Mormon Church. Smith and his family moved to southeast Wisconsin in 1835.

In 1843, Strang moved to Burlington, Wisconsin. Moses Smith was now living in Nauvoo, Illinois, the then capital of the Mormon religion; Moses' brother, Aaron Smith, resided in Burlington.

Not long after Strang arrived in Burlington, he accompanied Aaron Smith to Nauvoo. Strang soon adopted the Mormon faith and was ordained as an elder. He was given authority to found a

Mormon settlement near his Wisconsin home of Burlington. He named his new town Voree and told his followers it meant "garden of peace." He was held in high regard by his followers, though he enforced strict rules which included condemning material possessions, forbidding the eating of meat, and holding the sexual morality of his followers to his high standards. Accounts of the time show no internal strife in the settlement; however, external strife would soon change everything.

A year later, in 1844, an Illinois mob murdered Joseph Smith, the founder and Prophet of the Mormon Church, along with his brother, Hyram.

Strang rushed to Illinois with a letter saying Smith wanted him to be his successor. The Council of Elders was skeptical; the letter was supposedly written just days before Smith was murdered.

Brigham Young was elected Prophet shortly after. He promptly excommunicated Strang, who returned to Wisconsin with a number of Illinois Mormons. In Voree, Strang was referred to as Prophet until his death.

Strang's biggest achievement is the discovery of three metallic plates as a result of a divine vision. His followers went to the "Hill of Promise," dug beneath the base of a tree and uncovered the plates. Strange hieroglyphics covered both sides of the plates, which measured two feet by one foot.

Strang translated the plates, which he said were the records of "Rajah Manchore of Vorito." The message: "The forerunner, men shall kill, but a mighty prophet there shall dwell. I will be his strength, and he shall bring forth thy record. Record my words and bury it in the Hill of Promise."

Mounting hatred against the Mormons in Voree abruptly caused Strang and his followers to move to Beaver Island at the northern end of Lake Michigan—which coincidentally marked the beginning of the end for the town of Voree. Strang told his followers that the island was to become a kingdom and he was to become its king. Wearing a red velvet robe and a metal crown, 400 of his followers sang hosannas as Strang was crowned King James.

In 1850, Strang instituted polygamy, saying the Lord had commanded him to do so. Though not all of his followers embraced polygamy, Strang had five wives, including two teenage sisters.

Oddly, Strang soon began using violence to enforce his commands, and in 1856, two of his subjects shot him. Near death, two of Strang's young wives (four of whom were reportedly pregnant at the time) took him to his parents' home in Voree. It would be his final "homecoming."

This beautiful home near the White River, aka The River of Death, is still standing. When capturing the home on film, orbs are commonplace. Some of my photos taken during the daytime of Strang's death place and the River of Death show strange white marks. Even on a sunny day, you get the feeling you are being watched when you are near the property and the river.

Jesse James Strang died on July 9, 1856.

The home where Strang died, the Burlington Cemetery where he is buried, as well as the area where the plates were unearthed, are all considered haunted by those who visit them.

Photos taken in these places often reveal orbs. Some report a sick feeling in the pit of their stomach when they are in the area where the plates were discovered; I experienced a peaceful feeling, tempered with the feeling of being watched. The woods where the plates were discovered are among the most beautiful I've ever seen.

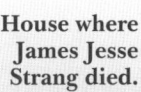

House where
James Jesse
Strang died.

No one is quite sure who the ghosts of Voree and Burlington represent. Are they Strang and his followers? Those who died during the Mormon/non-Mormon religious strife of the mid-1800s? The Native Americans who inhabited the area long ago, some of whom are buried in the twenty-seven burial mounds that lie beneath the Burlington area?

For some, it makes no difference. They say once you visit Voree and stand in front of the home where Strang died, the cemetery where he was buried, or near the marker denoting where the plates were unearthed, you will never be the same. The ghosts of Voree will remain with you always.

Marker commemorating discovery of plates.

Chapter 16
The Ghosts
Of Jefferson County

J efferson County is as haunted as any other county in south-eastern Wisconsin, and its ghosts are just as unique. First, there are the woods off Paradise Road in Jefferson. No one's quite sure what or who is haunting them, but something's going on there that defies explanation. Whoever enters, skedaddles out almost as quickly as they skedaddled in.

Then there's the small shadowy girl some have seen running along the bank of the Rock River. Is this the ghost of a little girl, whose body was found in the river?

And finally, the ghosts of the murdered and missing from the Concord House. I'll begin here.

The Concord House

The façade of the Concord House in Jefferson County might appear quite ordinary and harmless, at least as far as reception centers go. But its history and the feelings of unease you get once the sun goes down, tell a completely different story.

The belief that the Concord House is haunted stems from the fact that two very different, disturbing events took place outside the building: A high school girl disappeared from the premises during a prom party, and a teenage couple was found murdered after attending a wedding reception in the building.

Some experience a feeling of despair when they stand in the parking lot after dark. Others say the feeling is identical to the one they experience when they pass a stand of trees off Hustisford

Road, south of Highway 16 and the Canadian Pacific Railroad tracks. This is the spot where the decomposed bodies of the young couple were found two months after they left the Concord House, never to be seen alive again.

Do the ghosts of the murdered couple linger at the Concord House and the spot where their bodies were found? Are they, like their families and friends, waiting for a break in their case, now more than a quarter of a century old?

Or is the feeling of dread caused by the other ghost of the Concord House, the high school girl who left its doors, never to be heard from again?

The only thing known for certain, is the Concord House played an integral part in the two separate mysteries that are unsolved today.

The realization that the Concord might be haunted began months after the first tragedy. In June of 1974, Catherine Sjoberg, from Ixonia, disappeared during a prom party held at the Concord House. Catherine was seventeen years old and a senior at Oconomowoc High School. She had her whole life in front of her.

On that fateful day, Catherine had a disagreement with her date. At some point, she walked away from the Concord House and vanished. Her date was questioned, but passed a number of lie detector tests. It was as if she disappeared into thin air.

The second case attached to the Concord House, a double homicide, involves Timothy Hack and Kelly Drew, both nineteen years old at the time, who were attending a wedding reception there on August 9, 1980.

Many people at the reception saw Kelly and Tim walk to the exit, but this is where the story becomes a mystery. At some point, Kelly and Tim left the building, but no one that was questioned remembered seeing them leave.

Some speculate that a drifter or serial killer exited Interstate 94, took County Road F the short distance to the Concord House, and abducted the couple. Other speculation involves something more intimate. Did someone who knew Tim or Kelly abduct them and commit the murders?

Though both cases are cold cases, there is still hope that someone might come forward with information. Until then, the feelings of fear and anger associated with the Concord House will most likely continue...

Rock River

The Rock River that meanders through Jefferson County isn't known solely for its bountiful recreational activities. A little girl ghost has been seen frolicking along its banks.

At first the little girl looks real. But when you notice she's alone and go to her, she vanishes. Some speculate this small ghost is a girl, who disappeared on October 13, 1981.

The little girl's body was found nearly a month later. Though her death was ruled an accidental drowning, one investigator made a shocking assertion: a cult was responsible for her death. In addition, he believed the cult was responsible for other deaths in the area.

No one knows for sure who the little girl ghost seen along the banks of the Rock River is. If the little ghost was the victim of foul play, she doesn't appear to know it. She looks like any other little girl having a good time...

Paradise Road

Another haunted spot in Jefferson County is Paradise Road. Those that have ventured into the woods on the left-hand side of the woods say they feel an "eerie presence" that is hard to put into words.

The woods on Paradise Road are just past Saint Coletta's, outside the city of Jefferson. Many people—and not just kids—that have entered the woods have felt an "evil" or "creepy" presence on the left-hand side. Nothing anything odd or frightening seems to occur on the right-hand side.

Even during the day, you feel a ghostly interaction. When you take photos and videos, you might not think you're capturing anything, but when you take a closer look, wavering streaks and orbs can often be seen.

At night, if you're brave enough to venture into the left-hand side of the woods—and hopefully not alone—you'll undoubtedly hear footsteps. At least you'll hear what you believe to be footsteps. Some visitors to the woods have heard things dropping all around them. A ghost or ghosts having a little fun? Or is this a warning? Everyone that goes into the woods (the left-hand side) on Paradise Road believes the noises and feelings they get at night are a sort of "warning" from the unearthly inhabitants to leave them alone.

Another thing that can't be readily explained are the shadows that move past you. They do not come from any source, they are as big as a human, and are truly scary.

Visitors to the woods also say that no matter how frightening the experience, they want to come back again.

Which is fine. The ghosts of Jefferson County will be there.

Chapter 17

Four Ghosts...or More?

Luckily, Trudy Blakely isn't afraid of ghosts. She has three that share her living quarters full-time and a friend that stops in to pay a visit like she did when she was alive.

The three full-time ghosts that live in Trudy's apartment on Pine Street in downtown Burlington include a little boy about six years old, a little girl, and a woman.

A woman and girl's bones were found right next door. But that's probably not all that's underneath the area the building sits on. There's a boarded up entrance that is believed to lead to a tunnel Trudy has yet to explore.

Unlike many of us, she actually thinks about going through the doorway to see what lies behind it. The fuse box is in the basement, too, but so far, that's been the extent of Trudy's exploration.

Maybe it's a good thing she hasn't taken the boards off the door and taken a gander. The town of Burlington sits on a maze of tunnels that are said to contain unearthly beings.

An interesting bit of trivia about the town: It is now built on much higher ground than it was at one time. If you take a walk down the side streets, you can see doorways that look like basement entrances that were actually once first-floor entrances.

So it's very possible the other side of the door of Trudy's apartment basement could hold a surprise unlike any other. Burlington also is known for its sightings of strange creatures emerging from tunnel entrances. For now, sharing her apartment with the ghosts she's familiar with is enough.

The little girl and boy that reside with Trudy are "happy" ghosts. All they do is giggle. She never hears evil laughter that would make her want to break her lease. When Trudy hears mumbling—which could be either the girl or boy, or both—she smiles. "They're just talking to each other," she says.

Like many other ghosts, the ghosts that share Trudy's apartment do more than talk. She feels their presence when they're in front of her face. Shadows move through the apartment when there's no reason for a shadow to exist. Then there's the breathing on the back of her neck. But that's not all.

Trudy's friend, Karen, passed away recently, but only in human form. Sometimes when Trudy is on the computer, which is in her bedroom, she feels Karen sitting on the edge of the nearby bed, just like she used to do when she was alive.

Some might chalk this up to wishful thinking, but even Trudy's cat reacts to Karen's presence like it did when Karen was alive.

Whenever Karen stops by for a visit, the cat's hair will stand on end and it will hiss. If Trudy were alone, her cat would never hiss. The cat only hisses when someone else is around.

The cat's sensitivity to the ghostly presences in the apartment doesn't end there. It stands in front of the shower and stares at it, as if watching someone. When you pull the shower curtain back to see what it's looking at, there's no one there. At least no one you can see.

The apartment literally screams "haunting." Lights dim and get bright by themselves. The TV that is left on all the time will sometimes shut off by itself. It's a busy place.

It could just be the apartment itself is conducive to ghostly interaction; Trudy has recurring dreams in which her grandmother pays her a visit. These dreams are so real that Trudy will sometimes ask, "Grandma, how can you be alive?"

In addition to the cold spots throughout Trudy's living area, there's a place on the stairs that her cat avoids at all costs. Trudy thinks this is when the little boy ghost is sitting on the steps. The cat will hit a certain point on the stairs and then race back into the apartment—usually when Trudy hears the little boy talking or mumbling.

This might be enough to drive the average apartment dweller to seek new furnishings, but not Trudy. While she admits she might be more freaked out if she lived in the country, she says living in the city with people everywhere somehow makes her feel safe.

"As long as they don't hurt me, I don't care if ghosts are around me," Trudy says.

Plaque at Joan of Arc Chapel, Marquette University.

Chapter 18

Ghost Stone

Can a stone be haunted?

You may be inclined to say yes when you touch the so-called haunted Joan of Arc stone located inside the Medieval Chapel at Marquette University.

The stone doesn't wail or make unearthly sounds. It doesn't make the hair on the back of your neck stand on end (at least not until you touch it). And it doesn't make you want to flee the chapel. The rock does make you think about the woman, dead hundreds of years, who touched this rock.

Legend has it that a statue of the Virgin Mary sat on this very stone as Joan of Arc prayed just before she was burned at the stake.

That in itself is probably enough to make this particular stone magic, holy, or haunted—but as Joan of Arc rose from her meditation, she is said to have kissed it. Ever since, the stone has been cool to the touch, even when all else around it is warm.

Here's a little background about Joan, the haunted stone, and the chapel. As many of you might remember from history class, Joan of Arc was not an American. Jeanne d'Arc, was a young French woman who lived from 1412 to 1431. She was beatified in 1909 and canonized as a saint in 1920. Joan of Arc is a national heroine of France and was known as la Pucelle (the Maid) to those closest to her.

Joan was a devout Catholic. When she was about thirteen years old, she began hearing the voices of what she believed to be saints. Among these saints: St. Margaret, St. Michael, and St. Catherine. These voices told Joan that she was to become France's savior in the Hundred Years War, which had begun in 1337. The voices told her, "You must go! You must go!" She did.

Joan passed tests to establish her validity and mounted a campaign against the English. She fought her way successfully to Reims, where Charles VIII was finally crowned King of France. Shortly thereafter, she was captured by the Burgundians and sold as a prisoner to the English, who immediately attempted to have her sentenced for heresy and witchcraft.

While she was a prisoner of war, she attempted several unsuccessful escapes, including leaping from a seventy-foot tower into a dry moat. Later, Joan was tricked into wearing men's clothing, and put on trial. What was the reason she was eventually executed? Incredible as it may seem, the technical reason for her execution was a biblical clothing law. Wearing men's clothing was her undoing.

Joan of Arc was illiterate, but extremely intelligent. During her trial, she was asked if she was in God's grace, which was also a scholarly trap. She answered: 'If I am not, may God put me there; and if I am, may God so keep me.' Clever answer, but it was so much more. If she had answered yes, her words would have convicted her of heresy. If Joan had answered no, she would have, in effect, confessed her own guilt.

Too many factors were stacked against Joan at her trial; she was burned at the stake on May 30, 1431.

Twenty-four years later, the case was reopened by the French and Joan was acquitted. Hundreds of years later, the story of Joan of Arc still intrigues.

About the stone: after it was kissed by Joan of Arc, it eventually found its way to The Medieval Chapel, known as the Chapelle de St. Matin de Sayssuel. This chapel once stood twelve miles south of Lyons, France. It was built in the fifteenth century and later abandoned by the French. In 1927, it was moved to Long Island by Gertrude Gavine, the daughter of a U.S. railroad baron.

This very special stone was bricked into the wall to the left of the altar after being rebuilt.

The chapel moved again in 1965, this time to Marquette University, where it currently stands.

The stone is still cool to the touch. Don't believe it? All you have to do is place your hand on the vertical stone and then touch the base. You'll be able to tell the difference immediately.

St. Joan of Arc Chapel is located at Marquette University behind the Memorial Library. Admission is free.

This is one case where feeling is believing.

Joan of Arc Chapel, Marquette University.

Chapter 19

Kemper Hall and Durkee Mansion

Kenosha's Kemper Hall and Durkee Mansion are two brick buildings that are part of a complex of buildings that stand on 17.5 acres along Third Avenue on Lake Michigan's shore in Kenosha. The oldest building of the complex is the hauntingly beautiful Charles Durkee Mansion. It was built in 1861 and was the home of the original owner of the campus. Kemper Hall is a huge building once known as St. Claire Hall. The complex of buildings is now known as Kemper Center.

In the mid-1860s, the complex fell under the ownership of the Episcopal Church. In about 1871, it became a private Episcopal seminary for girls. Twenty years later, the science hall was outfitted with all the latest scientific equipment, such as Bunsen burners and a refractor telescope. This might not sound like a big deal, but it was almost unheard of in the 1800s to use this type of facility for women's studies. An interesting bit of Kemper Center trivia: Thomas Edison's great-granddaughter attended school here.

The main ghost story (it's gruesome) surrounding Kemper Hall involves a ghost nun, but has two very different versions.

The Falling Nun

The first version involves a telescope and a headless nun.

A nun by the name of Mother Mary Terese was said to be a cruel taskmistress who disliked the student body as a whole. She fell down the five-story spiral staircase inside the domed observatory where the telescope was housed. Some of her students then finished her off by pushing her out of a window.

Here's the same story, different slant. Others say several students were lying in wait for Mother Mary Terese, who was carrying an armload of books she had just retrieved from the observatory. These students shoved her down the stairs. She fell with such violence that her head was severed from her body before she reached the floor. Her head then thumped down the few remaining stairs and landed on her bloody black habit. Though records indicate Mother Mary Terese was never at Kemper Hall, it hasn't stopped this particular story from making the rounds.

The following story about someone who actually lived at Kemper seems more likely. Around 1878, the Sisters of St. Mary took over the seminary under the leadership of Sister Margaret Clare. She was said to be stern, just like Mother Mary Terese in the previous story. In this version, however, Sister Margaret Clare either tripped on her habit and fell, or was pushed to her death from the domed observatory tower. The truth is, Sister Margaret Clare died in 1921, the result of a chronic illness.

Suicidal Sister

The next ghost story tied to Kemper Center is about a student who committed suicide. What makes this story remarkable is that the suicide and ensuing cover up are well-documented.

The suicide took place at Kemper Hall in 1900. Sister Augusta, from Chicago, was attending an annual retreat at the seminary. She vanished without a trace, leaving behind her handbag, crucifix, and insignia of holy Sisterhood.

The authorities were alerted, and telegrams were sent to Chicago and St. Louis, where her family lived. On January 5, Kemper Hall issued a message to newspaper reporters and police—which were blatantly false—Sister Augusta was safely in Springfield, Missouri.

On January 8, Sister Augusta's lifeless body, still in her black robe, was found floating in the water near the beach at the east end of Seminary Street.

The following inquest revealed Sister Augusta's strange behavior before the suicide, all of which had all been covered up by Kemper Hall administration. Testimony revealed Sister Augusta had become "mentally deranged" from her work and had been granted time off. No one knows why she decided to end her life. Some speculate that she was heartbroken over a love she left behind.

Two young girls were the last to see her alive; they saw her walking along the beach the night of January 2.

Sister Augusta's death was ruled a suicide and she was laid to rest in her habit. Though her body was taken to St. Louis and buried in Bellefontaine Cemetery, could she be the ghostly nun seen moving about Kemper Hall in recent years? Many nuns are buried nearby; any one of them could haunt Kemper Hall.

Ghostly Activity

Sightings of ghosts at Kemper have been reported for over seventy years. One witness saw a female ghost who was wearing a brown dress. Other witnesses have seen shadows flit past them, accompanied by the sound of hurrying footsteps.

There have been countless reports of camera malfunctions, screams coming from empty rooms throughout the hall, and dark figures visible in windows of unoccupied rooms.

The Durkee Mansion, which has been preserved as a historical museum is also the site of continuous paranormal activity. The ghost of a nun who perished in a fire is said to float about the third floor. Dark figures can be seen in the windows of unoccupied rooms.

Paranormal investigators agree there is something strange going on at the Kemper Center. Whether it's because of "pent-up psychic energy" or the ghostly wanderings of nuns who are no longer alive, it's anyone's guess.

We do know, however, that Kemper Hall continues to be home to some very high levels of paranormal activity.

Recently, two sisters in their thirties attended a wedding at the Center. Not only did they hear disembodied screams, they took pictures of the grounds that later revealed many orbs. Neither sister knew beforehand about the Center's reputation for being haunted; both left Kenosha thinking the Center was the most unsettling place they had ever been.

Kemper Hall is located at 6501 Third Avenue in Kenosha.

Chapter 20

Pepé

If your house was built in 1901, chances are it probably does its share of creaking, moaning, and groaning. If you have an old house inhabited by a ghost, chances are you'll really get an earful—and eyeful.

Kathy Orndorf didn't expect her house in Burlington to include ghosts, but now that she knows about them, she's not about to move. That's because the ghosts that live with Kathy, her husband, and daughter, Brianna, are jokesters—even if the ghosts' pasts are nothing to joke about.

Brianna was the first to realize a ghost or ghosts shared their living quarters. Children are often more perceptive than adults because they more readily accept what they see and feel, instead of what they are told they are seeing or feeling.

Kathy used "Psychic Circle" to learn more about the ghostly inhabitants of her home. She also consulted a human ghost psychic. The information she learned was shocking, to say the least. Pepé, the biggest ghostly presence in the house, was a slave in the 1800s. He was a "master" slave and was beaten to death when he refused to do what his owner requested him to do. One can only wonder what the request was. Perhaps someday Pepé will reveal the answer.

Brianna has the biggest connection with Pepé. Pepé enjoys teasing Brianna by moving her things somewhere else and then putting them back after she's searched for them for a while.

The ghost psychic told Brianna that Pepé's favorite pet is the Orndorfs' pit bull pup. The family also has cats and other dogs. The older Rottweiler growls a lot at nothing, while the other pets freak out about nothing. Is Pepé teasing the Orndorfs' pets? Or is it a different ghost?

Footsteps are often heard outside the bedroom doors when no one else is home, and cold spots are prevalent throughout the entire house. Brianna's bedroom closet is always the coldest spot in the house. Kathy wonders if the closet isn't a portal.

The lights in the house also flicker for no reason and like many other haunted houses, the TV turns on and off for no reason.

Kathy has no doubt ghosts exists. She thinks back and realizes that she, like many other people, had ghostly encounters when she was young, but didn't know what they really were then.

Kathy has a theory about those who insist ghosts don't exist, "A lot of people who say they don't believe in ghosts or spirits are often those who had an experience when they were young that they couldn't explain, or an experience that frightened them. They try to block out these experiences so they won't come back to haunt them later." Makes sense to me.

One of the most recent ghostly experiences at the Orndorf residence involves Kathy and Brianna.

Kathy had just finished working. She and Brianna were standing at the kitchen sink at about 12:30 a.m., when a bright light moved past them. When they turned to follow it, the human-sized light moved across the living room and then disappeared from sight.

Kathy asked Brianna what she saw. They both agreed they had seen the same thing—a bright moving shape. At first they tried to attribute it to a car light. They quickly moved to the living room window to see if someone had just driven by, but the night was black and still.

Though Kathy, Brianna, and their pets are witness to constant signs of ghostly activity in the house, they wouldn't have it any other way. Life would be boring without their unseen houseguest(s).

As far as Pepé goes, he's shown no signs of wanting to move on; Kathy and Brianna share the sentiment.

After all, how many people can say they have a ghost like Pepé living with them?

Chapter 21
Old Buth Homestead

The specters of Mary and Marie Buth live on no matter how many people try to prove or disprove the stories that feature the two women. Some believe the Germantown homestead is dangerous...and haunted...while others say the story of the tragedies that took place there are just that, tragedies. Still, the stories continue to bring the curious to the old Buth Cemetery, even though it is surrounded by private property and not accessible to the general public.

Not long ago, several youths were arrested in the cemetery for trespassing; they were carrying knives for self-defense. Apparently, they imagined knives would help ward off any ghosts they might encounter. And this hasn't been the only trespassing incident. Another time, six trespassers were kicked out of the old Buth family cemetery after 11:00 p.m.

It's likely most of the curious go to the Buth homestead to see the woman dressed in gothic, translucent white clothing (or long, dark dress, depending on the account) reported to have been seen standing near the Buth home, or to hear the crying sounds that come from an upstairs bedroom when the home is deserted. When all is said and done, though, the only scare some trespassers get is meeting up with the Germantown Police.

Stories began in the 1960s when an intelligent, well-regarded resident of the old Buth farmhouse claimed he saw the figure of an old woman staring inside the house as he and his family were getting ready to celebrate the arrival of the New Year. The date: December 31, 1965.

The next day, the man looked at the plant near the window where the ghostly woman had been standing. The side of the plant that had been facing the apparition now sported wilted leaves; the leaves facing the inside of the house were healthy and green. The story triggered a wave of interest in the less than crystal history of the Buth homestead.

A few things are clear. The cemetery, besides being landlocked by private property, was quitclaimed to the Germantown Historical Society. Thirteen people are buried in the cemetery. And nearly all of those buried in the plot died prematurely or tragically.

Heinrich Buth, born in 1800, was killed by a falling tree in 1840. Heinrich's brother, Johann, was married to Marie. In 1841, Johann and Marie lost a son, about five years old, and a daughter, about three years of age, to sickness.

In 1845, Heinrich Buth lost a nine-year-old son. Then, in 1846, his seven-year-old daughter died. The death of an eleven-year-old girl, a baby, and another girl who is believed to have died in a house fire, each add to the number of bodies laid to rest in the cemetery.

Marie Buth's headstone indicates that she was born in 1807 and lived more than ninety years. Marie had six children; the youngest, Mary, who was born in 1850, lived into the twentieth century.

According to those who knew daughter Mary, she was a kind lady who had many cats. Mary was said to have lived a nice, ordinary life. After her last brother died, Mary went to live in Milwaukee. She died in 1926 and is buried in Germantown.

A psychic who visited the house, however, said she detected two ghosts in the house, and considered Mary an "evil" entity. Legend has it that Mary was left at the altar. Is she still waiting for the man who jilted her to return to her childhood home?

Residents of the house say the house and cemetery are not haunted. Others disagree. They swear they've seen a ghostly woman at the house and on the farm grounds. They cite the tragedies that took place there, and believe the entire homestead could not be otherwise.

Chapter 22

The Farmer

The ghost that inhabits the old farm on a sparsely traveled county road not far removed from the heavy traffic of Interstate 43 in New Berlin, is very much like the man he used to be: a loner, yet friendly.

The weathered barn seemed to be the farmer's favorite place in life. It's now his favorite place in death; perhaps because it's where he ended his life.

The reclusive farmer is remembered by his neighbors as a smiling man who always had his collie at his side. He always had a friendly wave for you as you passed his farm. If he wasn't walking out of his barn, you knew you would see him near his few cattle and horses.

Those that drove by each day knew exactly what time it was by the task the farmer was performing. He even walked out to his mailbox at exactly the same time each day to get his mail.

The farmer's orderly life apparently held secrets no one will ever know.

One night, a neighbor woman returning home from work, saw police cars lined up around the beautiful weathered barn. Some had their weapons drawn; some were inching their way inside.

Her imagination went into overdrive. New Berlin wasn't exactly the crime capital of North America. Perhaps the farmer had cornered someone inside the barn he had caught stealing from him. Or maybe he'd found a squatter in the hayloft and called the police to have him or her removed. The thought that the farmer had hung himself wasn't even a possibility. But that's exactly the reason the police were at the barn that evening.

The farmer that had always smilingly waved to her on her way to work and back would never wave to her again. Or so she thought...

Soon after the farmer's death, the cattle and horses disappeared from the farm. Weeds overtook the yard. Blinds covered the windows of the quaint two-story farmhouse. "For Sale" signs appeared in various places on the property. The farmer apparently had no family. And if he did, they didn't want the responsibility of a farm. Or maybe the farm now held too many bad memories, or came with a financial obligation the farmer's family couldn't handle. It was anyone's guess.

Summer turned to autumn, then winter, then spring. The acreage, including the barn, was sold. A short time later, the house began to show signs of being lived in. A different dog guarded the house. The lawn got mowed. Sometimes a car was parked outside the house.

The neighbor woman couldn't get the farmer out of her mind. He'd been such a nice, friendly man. She wished she had known a little more about him; if she had, perhaps she could have prevented the tragedy.

She knew it was foolish to waste her time thinking these thoughts, but the farmer reminded her of her own father.

One day that summer, as she was driving past the farmer's mailbox—now someone else's—she saw him walking to the mailbox to retrieve his mail, just as she'd seen him do a hundred times.

She swerved off the road, but managed to come to a stop just before she went into the ditch.

It was the farmer! As she stared at him, he waved at her just the way he always did. Shaken, she looked ahead to see if any traffic was coming toward her. When she looked behind her, the farmer was gone.

Since then, she's seen him walk toward his barn two more times. Each time he's disappeared into thin air. For whatever reason he chose to end his life, death apparently could not keep the farmer from the land and barn he loved in life.

The neighbor keeps a wary eye out for the farmer. When she sees him on that odd occasion, she doesn't feel sorry for him like she did when she first learned about his death; she's happy he's back at the farm.

Chapter 23

Brumder Mansion Bed & Breakfast

Want to see a ghost, but aren't keen on mucking through miles of mud to reach some remote cemetery? Want to get a rush from a paranormal encounter, but aren't enthusiastic about slicing your way through yards of cobwebs in an attic filled with vermin skeletons?

Then you might want to spend a night at the beautiful, yet thoroughly haunted Brumder Mansion Bed & Breakfast on Milwaukee's North Side.

Brumder is a big, gorgeous brick mansion in the downtown area. If you like a blend of Victorian, Arts and Crafts, and Gothic-style architecture, it's breathtaking to look at. If you like ghosts, staying here could take your breath away.

A female ghost named Aunt Pussy—yes, Aunt Pussy—is the fussy resident haunter. She's been known to tamper with window treatments and table settings; apparently she likes things decorated her way, and her way only.

George Brumder, a prominent Milwaukee businessman, built the mansion for his oldest son in 1910. After the Brumders moved out of the mansion, it became a boarding house, parsonage, and activity center for the Lutheran Church—not necessarily in that order.

The current owner of Brumder Mansion, Carol Hirschi, purchased the building in 1977 and began renovations. In 1978, Brumder Mansion Bed & Breakfast opened for business, complete with exquisitely-appointed rooms. To check it out before you check in, take a look at the Web site: http://www.brumdermansion.com/.

If you stay with a dog, however, you might find yourself enjoying the stay more than your canine companion. Aunt Pussy seems to dislike dogs. Perhaps Aunt Pussy was a cat person in another life?

The theatre is one of Aunt Pussy's favorite haunts; the ghostly lady has been seen there by a number of guests. Before the theatre was the theatre, it was a billiards room and a coffee shop called The Catacombs in the 1960s. Today, the Cornerstone Theatre Company holds professional productions and master acting classes in the theatre, located on the lower level.

Aunt Pussy's room in life was the beautiful "Gold Suite." It's another place you might see the ghost.

But paranormal activity inside the bed & breakfast's beautiful walls isn't limited to ghostly sightings. One time, Carol went to check on the Gold Suite which had been unoccupied for several days. She found fresh blood in the bathtub.

This most likely didn't unnerve Carol. The multi-talented woman has also co-produced and appeared in the movie, Wisconsin Death Trip.

Paranormal investigators researching the home also found a lot of "activity" in the bathroom, and guests who stay in the Gold Suite often tell of having vivid and odd dreams.

Adding to the bed & breakfast's intrigue: in Octobers past, guests have been greeted for a night of fright, complete with a séance held in the billiards room. *Haunted Times Magazine* sponsored Ghost Hunter University 101 and 102 at Brumder in September, 2007.

The *Haunted Times'* event might be the last haunted function Carol attends. When I spoke to her via phone, she said she was thinking about moving to Texas. As you might imagine, this has caused Aunt Pussy to express her displeasure.

Carol says, "My boyfriend hears Aunt Pussy call out my name and has seen her." Aunt Pussy isn't a threatening presence. "She doesn't pester us," Carol adds.

There have been about four investigations held at the mansion in the past three years. In that time, the paranormal activity in the house has not dropped off.

Carol's dog has been acting "really weird" in the middle of the night lately, too. The dog often wakes them up around midnight. Her dog also barks at nothing (at least nothing Carol or her boyfriend can see).

Carol, being the considerate host, has asked if the ghost would like to accompany her to Texas. The answer Aunty Pussy gives when asked—a resounding NO!

A psychic who recently visited the mansion told Aunt Pussy that if she didn't want to accompany Carol to Texas, she would help her cross over. The psychic's pendulum began swinging wildly and the front door opened on its own and slammed shut. If Aunt Pussy is one thing, it isn't subtle.

So if you want to rub shoulders with a very opinionated ghost in the very best of settings, give Carol a call.

Chapter 24

Seven Bridges Road

Seven Bridges is the locals' nickname for Jay Road in Bolton-ville. The locals also have another nickname for it: "Ghost Road."

Driving the entire length of this road may take a little gas, but even if you don't see one of the few "regular" ghosts along the way, or the bleeding stop sign, you're guaranteed to see some of the most beautiful scenery Wisconsin has to offer.

The first of Seven Bridges' ghosts is a young female jogger. It's said while she was jogging along a curve in the road, a drunk driver lost control of his vehicle and hit her. Adding more tragedy to the story—her body was never recovered from the swamp that runs alongside the road because the driver that struck her never reported the accident.

The Jogger

Those who believe in ghosts and even those who aren't sure if they do or not, have seen the misty figure of the young female jogger. This in itself would be a frightening event. But for some, this is only the beginning.

One couple told me that when they saw the jogger jogging down this particularly dark and creepy section of Seven Bridges Road, she looked so real that for a moment they braked to avoid hitting her. That's when she turned around and faced them!

When they "hit" her and she disappeared, the couple said they wished they'd brought an extra pair of underwear with them.

What makes this Seven Bridges ghost so unique is that she didn't make a solo appearance and disappear for good. She's been seen numerous times, and continues to be seen.

A Flying Bicycle

Another lesser known story involves a ghostly young boy on a 50s-style bicycle. The boy appears out of nowhere and then flies, with his bicycle, off the road into the ditch. No one remembers a young boy being killed here while riding his bicycle down this particular stretch of road, but the event might have taken place long ago.

Cats Aplenty

The third Seven Bridges ghost story also features a female ghost; but this one is much older. This old lady lived on Seven Bridges Road, alone, except for dozens of cats who turned out to be much better friends than the kids in the area.

These kids, let's just call them what they were—bullies—started out by taunting the old woman at night. Did she yell at them to stay off her property and say she was going to call the police? It's safe to say she might have been frightened enough to do either. Who knows—maybe the old woman's threats caused the war between her and the kids to escalate. Regardless, the kids began killing her cats. And the nightmare didn't stop there.

One night the old woman's house caught fire; some say the kids started it. The old woman, instead of fleeing the fire, stayed inside and died in the burning building.

Her ghost is said to walk alongside the road near where her house once stood. Sometimes a ghost cat or two accompany her. One can only speculate whether she's looking to chase the local kids away from her house, or just looking for more of her cats.

If you drive down Seven Bridges Road today, chances are good you'll see stray cats. These cats are said to be descendants of old woman's cats. I saw several tan cats at different locations along the road. They seemed timid, as if afraid to be seen.

A Bleeding Stop Sign

Besides ghosts, the road has a stop sign that bleeds. This unique sign is located at the intersection of Boltonville Road and County Road SS. It appears to be bleeding as you approach it, especially late at night when your headlights are shining on it. But when you stop and get out, the stop sign suddenly stops bleeding, and there's no sign of blood.

If you're like me, you might wonder why a stop sign would bleed. Here's the story: Rumor has it a man living in a house near the stop sign brutally murdered his wife.

Adding to the fear factor—when you are stopped at the stop sign, you might hear footsteps approaching, though no one is there. You might also hear Native American song (the murderer is said to be Native American).

Intrigued? Jay Road, or Seven Bridges Road, begins in Boltonville and runs through Ozaukee and Washington Counties.

The marshy part of Seven Bridges where the jogger was reportedly killed is about two miles outside of Boltonville in Washington County. And yes, there are seven bridges on Seven Bridges Road.

Chapter 25

Twin Lakes Rental

Rental units are not in short supply in Twin Lakes; either are units that come with an invisible roommate. Two rental houses that were once part of a nursing home complex are known to be haunted.

This is a story about one rental house in particular. Two different renters have two very different ways of remembering their stay in this house, though both renters have no doubt the house is haunted.

The first renter moved out because she didn't like living with ghosts. She wouldn't have signed the lease had she known a ghost or ghosts were already residing there, but once she was there, she tried to make the best of it. At first she chalked up all the strange occurrences to stress. But then some things happened that made her realize she wasn't imagining having ghosts in her house. She also realized the ghosts that were living with her didn't like her very much.

Never mind the intense feeling of being watched and the "bad" feeling she got when she was alone. The ghosts of this rental house would go so far as to empty garbage out on her cupboard when she turned her back. That's not all; they moved things around and they messed with her mind.

As you might imagine, it got old in a hurry. The renter packed up and moved away, but not without telling the next renter about the ghosts that had made her life miserable.

The next renter, being the practical sort, wasn't put off by stories of ghosts. She needed a place to live that would accept pets and the house was within her budget. She promptly moved in.

It didn't take long before the new renter felt the ghostly presences just like the renter before her had. But unlike the first renter, she had no trouble with the ghosts. They were well-behaved; they actually seemed to like her. The second renter's ghosts left her things in place and didn't overturn any garbage. The one sore spot: the ghosts didn't like her pets as much as she did.

She could tell when a ghost was nearby by observing her pets' behavior. Her dogs especially avoided certain places in the house and acted strangely toward things she couldn't see. The renter's two lab-German shepherd-mix dogs did everything they could to stay out of the basement of the house. But when one of them was ready to give birth, the renter had no choice but to put the pregnant dog downstairs.

The moment the mother dog had her puppies and was strong enough to crawl up the stairs, she brought each puppy upstairs, shoving her body against the door so the renter couldn't bring the puppies back downstairs.

The dogs weren't the only animals to take note of the ghostly presence in the house. The renter's cat and bird also acted strangely when something unearthly was nearby. The renter remembers awakening one night to the sound of her bird singing. She kept it in a cage in a room across the hall.

How odd, she thought. The bird never sang in the middle of the night. The renter quietly and slowly opened her bedroom door. The instant she cracked the door open, her cat hurtled inside the bedroom and slid underneath the bed to hide.

Again the renter found this strange, but continued to the room across the hall where the bird was singing. When she got there, she was shocked to find the bird was fast asleep.

Feeling somewhat unsettled, she checked to make sure no one was in the house that shouldn't be, and then returned to her bedroom.

As she got into the bed and brought the covers up to her chin, her cat did something it never did before and would never do again: It dove beneath the covers and huddled against her as if seeking protection.

The renter figures the ghost was teasing her cat. Even so, no real harm done. The ghosts continued to make their presence known, but never in any malicious way. The renter moved out at the end of her lease, not one day sooner.

If you're looking for a nice rental house in the Twin Lakes area and don't mind a ghost with a sense of humor, you might want to check out these two rental houses. Otherwise, you might want to seek something a little more modern without the ghostly baggage.

Chapter 26

Angelynne's Uncle

Angelynne's uncle committed suicide when he was twenty-eight years old. It was a tragic end to a life that formerly was filled with laughter and promise.

Uncle Chris joined the Army out of high school and married two years later. When he came home, he was never the same. He used to "think 24/7 about what happened" while he was enlisted. He rarely mentioned his friends that had died alongside him, and tried to change the subject if someone brought up anything to do with the military; but his time in the service was never far from the forefront of his mind.

His wife and family thought he was suffering from depression, but he refused to seek medical help. The only thing that seemed to snap him out of his moods was his six-year-old niece, Angelynne.

When Angelynne asked her Uncle Chris to take her fishing or pull her in her wagon, he seemed to forget everything else, even if it was only for a few hours. Unfortunately, one day even Angelynne couldn't make him forget the ghosts of his past.

One seemingly ordinary day, Chris woke up, made a call to the police, and goaded them into shooting him. He had a water pistol in his hand.

Chris is remembered as being a wonderful husband, a friend who would do anything for you, and someone who wasn't afraid to try anything: skydiving, bungee-jumping...kayaking. He was a loving son who often checked in with his parents. And he was the best uncle ever.

If Chris had one regret, it was that he never had children of his own. He mentioned it every year when he spent the first week in July at the family's lake home, a short walk from Lake Michigan's shore.

Angelynne was young when she lost her uncle. Like all young children, she didn't seem to grasp the fact he would never pull her in her wagon again.

The family gathered together at the summer home like they did every first week in July, but things were different that time. There was little joking around; everyone was thinking about Chris.

Then, while eating lunch, Angelynne announced that Uncle Chris said he wished everyone could just have a good time. He was happy. Everyone stopped eating and stared at Angelynne's serious little face.

"What?" she asked with a shrug. "That's what he said." She picked up her sandwich and began eating as if she hadn't said a word.

It was a disturbing statement that made everyone wonder how Angelynne was really coping with the death of her beloved Uncle Chris, but no one said much about it at the time. Sometimes it's easier to push things out of our minds instead of talking about them. Who wants to open an even bigger can of worms than the one that's already open?

Two days flew by. Everyone seemed to forget Angelynne's lunch-time comments. That afternoon, Angelynne and her mother stayed inside the cabin because it was too windy to do much outside. They were going to fly kites when the wind died down.

While they waited, Angelynne sat in a chair in the corner, facing an empty sofa. She had a doll on her lap, but wasn't playing with it. Angelynne's mother and grandmother were sitting in chairs at the opposite end of the room; one knitting, the other doing a Sudoku.

"I wish you would," Angelynne said suddenly, still looking at the sofa.

Angelynne's mom and grandmother glanced at her, and then at each other. Angelynne said nothing more, so after a minute or two, the two adults resumed doing what they were doing.

"Uh-uh. She don't like to," Angelynne said again a moment later. "She don't do it right."

Mother and grandmother exchanged uneasy looks.

Suddenly Angelynne's face lit up. "Yay!" she said, running to the kitchen cabinet. She put her hand behind it and began searching for something.

"What are you doing?" her mother asked.

"Looking for what he got me."

"Who got you what?"

"Uncle Chris got me something. A s'prise." With that, she pulled out a paper bag that contained a small sticker book. "Pretty! Thank you," she said politely to the sofa.

Angelynne's mother quickly got up and went to Angelynne. "Who told you that was there?" she asked, her voice trembling.

"Uncle Chris," Angelynne said with a roll of her eyes, pointing to the sofa.

Both women glanced where she was pointing. No one was there.

Angelyne's grandmother dropped her knitting needle, "Who?" she whispered.

"Uncle Chris." She stared leafing through the little book. "He said we can fly kites now. It's not too windy."

They all looked outside. The sky was calm.

Chapter 27
Bay View Ghosts

Bay View is quaint, picturesque...and haunted.

    Scenic Bay View, just a stone's throw from the skyscrapers of Milwaukee proper, is a source of pride to those that live and work here. A little trivia about Bay View that you might not know: it also happens to be home to Milwaukee's last functioning artesian well. It's such a popular destination for those that want to fill their jugs with its water, that the Bay View Gardening and Yard Society has prettied up the area around the well with benches and potted plants.

    People who regularly visit the well to gather the iron-y tasting water swear it has curative powers. Some say it makes their plants grow bigger and stronger. Some say it helps them lose weight. Others visit artesian well for the most basic reason: to cool off on hot summer days. Which leads me smoothly into the first Bay View ghost, who happens to reside in a picture-perfect Cape Cod just a few blocks from the artesian well.

    Just like the people from Bay View, Ruthie the ghost is a friendly sort. She's believed to have had Alzheimer's when she was alive. She also kept her yard and garden, like the rest of her Bay View neighbors, neat as a pin.

    Surprisingly, it's not her neighbors—or the current residents of the house—who see Ruthie out in the garden, waving at them as they pass by. It's the neighborhood children, on their way home from a dunk in nearby Lake Michigan or a visit at a friend's house.

Ruthie, bent over "her" flowers, seems to sense when children race past on bicycle, skateboard, or on foot.

She will slowly straighten, and wave at them with a sweet smile. So how do the children know Ruthie's a ghost? The obvious answer: You can see through her.

The ghost in the garden is believed to be a woman who died twenty years ago. Strangely, she began making appearances in just the last couple of years. The kids who see Ruthie are stingy with the information they share because they "don't want to put a hex" on their relationship. They like the old woman and figure it's nice to have a "good" ghost keeping an eye on them on their way home from the lake.

Which might not be a bad thing. There are some rather scary ghosts in Bay View, and they're not that far away.

A stone's throw away (if you're Goliath) from Ruthie's house, is a huge recently rennovated building complex. It's known for being a haven for ghosts, and not the friendly variety.

The complex has been haunted for decades. Local musicians once rehearsed on the first and second floors of one of the old buildings. Some remember hearing unearthly noises and experiencing the feeling of something watching them. Critics, perhaps?

The buildings were vacant for years, like many other Bay View businesses (many of which are now being transformed into cafés and other commerce). When repairs were begun on this complex, however, many parts of the deep interior were ignored. This gave many ghost hunters the perfect opportunity to see if the rumors of ghostly habitation were true.

One group of amateur paranormal investigators said later they were lucky they weren't hurt walking around the sealed-off areas they should not have been exploring. Whole floors were rotted away. Piles of debris showed dozens of rodent skeletons tangled in ropes. Staircases had steps missing and were incapable of supporting weight. Mazes of dark rooms, accessible only from the hall, had no exit. Doors slammed shut for no reason. Ominous and unearthly noises from the depths of the building made those wearing crucifixes to clutch them until they cut into their fingers. Some said they prayed out loud.

Heavy footsteps and thin moans emanated from empty rooms. Shadows moved across the floor where there was no light to create a shadow.

Perhaps the most disturbing thing some stumbled across was a room in the bowels of one of the buildings, described as makeshift medical examination room. A table, complete with dried blood around it, stood in the center of the room. This might have been a legitimate medical examination room, or a convenient place to perform satanic rituals. It's anyone's guess. The blood stains may have been something worse, said one man who saw them. "The entire room smelled worse than death." Some say one room (might be the same room) contained a blood-covered saw leaning against one corner.

Others who ventured inside the building before renovations began also report hearing crying. One explorer heard whispering in her ear.

All I spoke to agreed these Bay View ghosts were the "angriest" and most "aggressive" ghosts they'd ever encountered.

Chapter 28

Ghost "Doc"

Many people have never heard of Milwaukee's very own Sherlock Holmes. Perhaps it's because he was born in 1866; perhaps it's because his incredible ability to crack unsolvable crimes didn't involve having to rely on physical evidence.

Those who are familiar with this talented man say he was psychic. Others say he talked to ghosts to help him solve cases.

Arthur Price Roberts was born in Denbigh, Wales. When he was a boy, he and his uncle moved to Fox Lake, Wisconsin. Roberts first became aware that he wasn't like other boys his age when he was in his teens. This is when he heard about a man who had lost some money. When he focused on the man, he immediately saw a picture of the hiding place of the money in his mind that proved to be true.

This was the beginning of a career that involved putting a lot of ghosts to rest.

Though it's hard to believe, Roberts was illiterate all of his life. He thought an education might destroy his unique abilities. His friends called him "Doc"; he did most of his puzzle-solving in Wisconsin, though he sometimes helped solve cases elsewhere in the United States.

One of Doc's more notable cases involved Duncan McGregor. The Peshtigo, Wisconsin, man had been missing for a number of months, and the police had hit a dead end. McGregor's wife asked Roberts to help.

Roberts went into a trance. He told Mrs. McGregor that her husband had been murdered, but couldn't say who was responsible because his testimony wouldn't be admissible in court. He did tell McGregor's wife that her husband's body could be found in the Menomonee River.

You guessed it. McGregor's body was found in the Menomonee River, just as Roberts said.

Another case involved wealthy Chicago financier, J. D. Leroy, who asked Roberts to find his brother who had disappeared while on a trip to Albuquerque, New Mexico, about six months earlier.

Doc Roberts told Leroy that his brother had been murdered and his body dumped in Devil's Canyon—all without having to leave his Milwaukee home. Doc added a description of the area where Leroy's brother's remains could be found. The corpse was recovered a few weeks later in Devil's Canyon, not far from the area Roberts described.

Doc also helped the Fond du Lac Police Department solve a murder case. He identified the killer—a member of the Royal Mounted Police, no less—again from the comfort of his home. The Canadians found the killer in Canada, working for the Mounties. The killer confessed.

In another case, Chicagoan Ignatz Potz was about to be executed in the electric chair. Potz's family asked Doc to help them. Potz admitted he was present at the killing he was convicted of, but said he took no physical part in it. Roberts investigated and came up with new evidence. This new evidence was key in having Potz's sentence commuted to life imprisonment.

Roberts biggest triumph, however, occurred in 1935. In October of that year, Roberts predicted Milwaukee would soon fall victim to a series of bombings. Days later, dynamite ripped a hole in the Shorewood Village Hall's foundation. The explosion was felt for blocks around the hall; area homes and offices were damaged. Then the Citizens Offices of the First Wisconsin National Bank and the East Side Offices of the First Wisconsin National Bank were hit. Explosions also rocked two police substations.

The police asked Doc for help. He told them the last explosion would take place on November 4, somewhere south of the Menomonee River. Unfortunately, he couldn't tell them who the criminals were or the exact spot where the explosion would take place.

Police followed Doc's instructions to the letter. They checked the entire area, but unfortunately missed a small shed. At 2:40 p.m. on Sunday, November 4, two young men began setting a timing device. They made a mistake and the shed, with an estimated forty sticks of dynamite inside, exploded. The two young men died, along with an innocent nine-year-old girl who happened to be in her second-story bedroom overlooking the shed when the blast occurred.

Doc's intimate association with the supernatural went beyond crime solving. In November, 1939, at a small dinner party given in his honor, Roberts said he wouldn't be with them beyond January 2, 1940. Doc Roberts died peacefully in his sleep on January 2, 1940. He was a man who did the best he could to help others; he did not seek fame or fortune.

Doc's amazing talents were proven time after time, but one has to wonder how many times the ghosts of the dead helped him solve cases believed by most to be unsolvable.

Chapter 29
Seven Bridges— Grant Park

Beautiful Grant Park is located along the shores of Lake Michigan. Consisting of 381 acres, this is the second largest park in the county's park system. It is also home to lots of paranormal activity, much of which occurs after sunset. This poses a problem because the park closes at 10:00 p.m. If you want to see any ghostly activity, make sure you park on a side street instead of inside the park. Otherwise, you might get a parking ticket to add to your night's experiences.

The main entrance bridge is thought to be the most haunted spot in the park. Several people are said to have committed suicide by jumping or hanging themselves. It's been reported that murders have also occurred in the vicinity of the bridge. The exact number of people who ended their earthly life in Grant Park is not known.

The view from the main entrance bridge is mesmerizing, especially if you look down into the ravine. The air above the ravine is often filled with dancing lights and orbs, visible to the naked eye and also on film. Many have seen lights in the woods. Others have seen a ghost woman slowly making her way along the bridge. This ghost is the most famous of Grant Park's ghosts. She's said to be looking for her two sons who drowned there.

Others say that if you stand on the entrance bridge, you might see a human-sized shape appear, or a mist that has a humanlike shape. Many believe these apparitions are suicide or murder victims.

Those who visit Seven Bridges between sunset and midnight report seeing lights coming from the depths of the woods. These lights are sometimes stationary; sometimes they move. If you venture into the woods to check out the lights, you might hear screaming and/or laughing of the disembodied nature.

This is usually enough to make you stop in your tracks. This is also when you'll hear something coming toward you. It will sound like a human, complete with heavy footsteps and heavy breathing—only there won't be anyone attached to the sounds.

Three teenage girls I spoke to said they've been to the park a "hundred times." On two occasions they saw strange lights. One time they heard screaming that was so "bone-chilling" that they left the park screaming their heads off.

Chapter 30

Eternal Circus

Delavan was once called the "Circus Capital of the World," in part because twenty-six circuses wintered here from 1847 to 1894. The famous P. T. Barnum Circus, called the "The Greatest Show On Earth," was founded in Delavan in 1871. The term, Circus Capital of the World, still applies in once sense: Delavan is the final resting place for dozens and dozens who made the circus their life.

New York brothers Edmund and Jeremiah Mabie brought their circus to Delavan in 1847. Apparently there was no maybe about it: Delavan's abundant pastures and water sources made it the ideal place to support circus horses and other animals. Animals, as you might imagine, were a nineteenth century circus' most important assets because they were used for transportation and performances.

The Mabie Circus stayed at the present site of Lake Lawn Resort on Delavan Lake, where it created a circus dynasty that survived in Wisconsin for the next 100 years. The International Clown Hall of Fame was organized in Delavan in 1987, and operated by a community museum until it moved to Milwaukee a decade later.

If you were a citizen of Delavan in the 1800s, you might see elephants grazing alongside horses and acrobats practicing maneuvers along the road. Circus members bought property in Delavan and infused the local economy, and the people of Delavan embraced their unusual neighbors.

Drive into Delavan today and you'll see what looks like a nice, ordinary town: beautiful old buildings, friendly people, and refreshing unpretentiousness. Drive a little further and you'll see Delavan isn't quite as ordinary as it first appears. Downtown, near the water tower are two life-size statues: one of a huge giraffe, and the other of one of the most famous elephants in history: Romeo. Look beneath Romeo's thrashing feet and you'll see a waving, oblivious clown.

Lest you think Romeo was the town hero, think again. Romeo was a killer. He killed five people during a fifteen-year period. He crushed, impaled, and trampled his victims to death, not unlike some of the elephants you hear about today. The one big difference between Romeo and the elephants of today is that killer elephants are quickly disposed of or removed to a spot where they can no longer hurt anyone. Romeo, on the other hand, was allowed to kill and kill again. Along with his murderous rampages, he also destroyed buildings. He nearly tore apart a theater in Chicago.

The statue of Romeo and the clown about to be trampled is on the north side of Walworth Avenue, between Main and Second Streets. Many members of the circus that called Delevan "home" are buried in Spring Grove Cemetery at the end of Seventh Street. About seventy members of the circus have been laid to rest here— sort of; some died violent deaths. Circus performers, clowns, and acrobats are said to come to "life" at night in the cemetery. Citizens of Delavan, as well as the curious, have seen ghost clowns and horses going about their business here.

Graves of the Delavan circus people can be easily identified by oval metal markers next to their headstones. Dozens of other circus members are also buried in St. Andrew's Cemetery.

One member of the circus in particular is thought to haunt his final resting place. Years ago, the Delavan Police reportedly shot circus manager, Joseph McMahon, because of a gesture he made to retrieve his handkerchief. The police thought he was going for a gun. Apparently, they knew McMahon and decided to play it safe rather than sorry. It worked. They were safe; McMahon was sorry.

Another of the graveyard's inhabitants, Dr. Upp (real name: R. A. Palmer), smashed into a brick hotel in Delavan a few months later. One of his guidelines apparently got snagged.

There are rumors of descendents of the circus, notably those "endowed" differently than the rest of us, still living in secrecy along the edge of Lake Delavan.

Lake Lawn Resort was built on the north shore of Lake Delavan in 1878 so members of the circus would have a place to stay. Ghostly circus workers have been seen in the area, performing tasks they performed when they were alive. This same area was occupied by Native Americans as early as 1,000 B.C. To this day, any renovations to the resort must be done carefully, to avoid disturbing the remaining burial mounds.

Guests of the hotel have reported seeing figures of Native Americans in "old-time" dress on the golf course. Sometimes these sightings are as plain as day; sometimes they are shadowy. Ghost circus workers and Native Americans aren't the only ghosts to have been spotted at Lawn Lake Resort. The ghostly sound of an elephant trumpeting has been heard. Could it be Romeo, the killer elephant? The owners of Barnum ordered workers to push Romeo (some accounts say it was actually Juliet, Romeo's partner) out to the middle of lake when he died. The lake was frozen at the time. When the ice thawed, Romeo sunk. There are those that swear they've seen a ghostly elephant trunk reach out of the water. And if there's one elephant just mean enough to come back from the dead, it would be Romeo.

Delavan isn't only known for its circus ghosts, it's home to Andes Candies™, maker of the delicious Andes Chocolate Mint. Andes has been in Delavan since 1921 and is still manufacturing here today.

Ghosts and chocolate. Could there be a better combination?

Chapter 31

Marquette University

Officials at the Catholic Jesuit University have a no comment policy regarding any ghosts that may haunt their beautiful old buildings.

But students and former students will tell you Marquette is alive with ghosts.

When most students name a haunted spot on campus, they nearly always mention Humphrey Hall first. This student dormitory was formerly the Milwaukee Children's Hospital.

The upper floors have been converted into student housing, but some parts of the lower floors, especially the lobby, look almost the same as when they served the hospital. The basement of the hall, when it was a hospital, housed the morgue. Though I could not find an exact number, many children are believed to have died here during the time Humphrey Hall was the Milwaukee Children's Hospital. Even after the hospital moved, children were seen on camera monitors in the building.

Two roommates who lived at Humphrey Hall, who wish to remain nameless, had more than one ghostly encounter. Their room was on what used to be Intensive Care, and it was remote from the other rooms because of the way the building is laid out. They said part of the dorm was also used for something other than housing, though no one ever found out what. Interestingly, light and motion sensors were always on, even in corridors that were off limits to students.

They said most of the halls were blue and gray, giving the hall a very "quiet" feel. Most of the occupants of the hall were seniors, which meant it had a calmer atmosphere. They rarely heard the loud music, fighting, or yelling that is typical in many other dorms.

The girls often heard running in the halls, but when either of them ran outside their dorm and pursued the sound, they saw nothing but shadows that disappeared into one of the closed off corridors. The motion and light detectors never went off in those corridors.

The sounds of distant screaming and crying were also common sounds. Both girls admit they were tempted to attribute the sound to fellow students who might have had a little too much to drink, but the sounds were thin and childlike and were likely to be heard during the daytime as well as during the night.

Like many other students in the hall, they saw the little girl ghost dressed in a white hospital gown that many have reported seeing. Another ghost others have reported seeing is called the "lost" ghost because she seems to wander aimlessly, as if hoping to stumble across the right room. Once the lost ghost is spotted, she flees and then vanishes—sometimes moving through solid doors. Now that's a memorable exit.

Several rooms in the building have very chilly spots in them that never go away. A breeze blows through these same rooms even when all doors and windows are closed and the rooms are not being heated or cooled.

The girls say they hid their empty crushed beer cans in a paper bag behind some books, underneath their desk. (They didn't say why.) They remember being freaked out when they came back to the dorm one night and found the beer cans all over the floor and every drawer and door inside the room open. No one else could have entered the room.

One of the girls had an even bigger scare. She was sleeping when something caused her wake up. She remembers it wasn't a sound; rather a feeling that she was being watched. She looked up and saw a small child looking down at her. When she realized she could see through it, she screamed loud enough to wake the dead. In this case, it was apparently enough to scare the dead. The child, after a moment or two, vanished into thin air. The girl swears it was a ghost. She said she "hadn't been dreaming, or drinking, or anything."

Others have seen the child ghosts, but most just hear childish laughter and screaming when no one's around.

Video security cameras that monitor the building's rear entrance sometimes capture the image of a ghostly young girl.

The Helfaer Theater on campus has a gruesome past. A projector operator, while on a smoking break near a huge ventilation fan in a hallway off the balcony, somehow snagged his clothing and was drawn into the fan. Though the ghost of the man who died has never been seen, he is thought to be responsible for lending assistance in the form of turning off lights and locking doors when others forget.

Another ghost with a bent for theatrics is a former artistic director who died in Studio 13 and has been spotted on the catwalks of the theater and in the studio itself.

Straz Hall, formerly East Hall, was once a YMCA. It also has a ghost—Whispering Willie. Legend has it the little boy drowned in the swimming pool. He's been seen swimming alongside other swimmers who are by themselves in the Rec Plex pool; perhaps keeping an eye on them to make sure they don't suffer the same fate.

Willie is as mischievous as any living boy. He opens and closes doors, unrolls toilet paper in bathrooms, and repeats others' words—in whispers, of course.

Cobeen Hall is Marquette's only all-female residence. Because the residents are first year students, it's a lively place. The ghost that resides there is also lively. If it takes a liking to a student, it will leave them alone. If the ghost takes a dislike to a student, it will repeatedly remove artwork from their walls.

Johnston Hall is also the site of paranormal activity. Whether it's because of the two Jesuit priests that reportedly threw themselves off the roof, or because Native American spirits are unhappy because the hall stands on burial ground, there's an unease that is felt by many who enter the building.

Students in this building have seen ghostly faces in fifth floor windows. Others get a strange feeling if they walk down a hall alone. Temperatures inside the building plunge for no reason, and cameras often stop functioning.

Newspaper staff once spent the night on the fifth floor. They heard voices and captured an image on film that defied explanation. They also reported the same chilly temperatures many experience feeling when they are on either the fourth or fifth floors.

Mashuda Hall, now recently renovated and free from ghostly presences, was once the site of some very frightening poltergeist activity. A student reported flying objects, frightening sounds, and writing on windows that were fogged-up. This was after a female student committed suicide in the hall. The paranormal activity didn't last long—a priest blessed the room and performed an exorcism. The frightening activity ceased and has never returned.

A number of other buildings on campus are also rumored to be home to ghosts.

Chapter 32

Fork In The Road Restaurant

The Fork In The Road is a two-story restaurant known for its charming atmosphere, cheerful service, great food... and haunting atmosphere.

This former tavern, once called Inn The Older Days, is located on North Rochester Street (Highway 83) in Mukwonago. It's easy to spot with its cheery yellow exterior and packed parking lot. The restaurant is famous for its "Mukwonago Kick" and fish fry.

At one time, Fork In The Road was also a thriving hotel. A fire supposedly burned down the hotel part of the building, but no one is known to have died.

Fork In The Road Restaurant. Mukwonago.

This makes it hard to know exactly who has taken up ghostly residence. Billiard balls have been heard chinking together and rolling along the floor. Footsteps can be heard making their way through the restaurant, though no one is there. Some have heard disembodied voices and seen fog in storage areas.

Two ghosts are believed to inhabit the restaurant. One is known as "The Captain" by some. The other ghost is seen upstairs. She is said to move between the main room and the dining room. Perhaps a former server or maid?

A frequent guest of The Fork In The Road said he would come to the restaurant because of the food and service anyway, but the in-house ghosts are an added attraction.

One time when he was dining upstairs, he put his fork down. A second later, it literally flew off the table. He asked for another fork. That one also flew off the table.

He now jokingly calls the restaurant, Fork On The Floor.

Chapter 33
North Point Lighthouse and Lion Bridges

North Point Lighthouse, located in Lake Park, is one of Milwaukee's oldest public parks. It's also said to have ghosts aplenty—of the juvenile variety.

The lighthouse was built to mark the entrance into the Milwaukee River. It was constructed of cream city brick and officially opened in November of 1855. In 1888, the original building was replaced and moved inland about 100 feet. Though much shorter at one time, it currently stands seventy-four feet tall.

Lion Bridges, not far from the North Point Lighthouse, are known for the two lions that sit at the end of each bridge. Paul Kupper sculpted the sandstone felines, which were later donated by the manager of the Milwaukee Electric Railway and Light Company.

The bridges were narrowed and closed to traffic in 1964. Shortly after, visitors began reporting seeing ghostly children standing sentinel near the lions. When they would get close to the lions, the children would run off and vanish into thin air.

To this day, ghostly children are spotted on the park grounds near the lighthouse, but especially near the lion statues.

Laugher, not the nice kind, is also heard in the park even when no one is around. Cold spots in the park and the overall feeling that you are not welcome are feelings many experience when they are there. Who are these children ghosts? No one has an explanation. People that see these ghostly children say they have a "menacing" aura about them.

This is one place that many Milwaukeeans mention when asked if they know any haunted spots. Some residents never return to Lake Park because of the very strong feeling (bad) they got when they were near the lion bridges.

Recent visitors to the bridges at night captured orbs "jumping off" one of the bridges.

No one can explain why there is such strong paranormal activity concentrated here. Even during the day, children ghosts can be seen and their presence felt.

Chapter 34

Peter Cooper Glue Factory

I magine an encounter with one ghost. Now try thirty.

Located in Oak Creek/Carolville, this factory has a long and strong reputation as a habitat for the no-longer living. It also has a history shrouded by mystery. Facts about deaths that supposedly took place there are nonexistent, or at the very least, very well-hidden. Research I've conducted has turned up little. Letters I've written to numerous agencies and organizations have gone unanswered. Even so, ghost hunters from all around Wisconsin flock to the abandoned building where scores of workers are rumored to have lost their lives (were murdered) while performing their duties.

What's amazing—or perhaps incredible would be a better word—is the absence of obituaries. But given the nature of the business, it seems entirely plausible that deaths did occur here—especially in the days before OSHA. Perhaps many deaths. One likely reason is the name itself. Peter Cooper Glue Factory might not be the factory's real name.

There once was a glue factory called United States Glue Works that was in operation in the early years of South Milwaukee. Could this be Peter Cooper Glue Factory's correct name? United States Glue Works is listed in historical books as being "well located for making use of bones, horns, hooves and other wastes from the packing plants from which they make glue, gelatin and fertilizer." During the time United States Glue Works was in business, South Milwaukee was also home to a tanning company and a "gelatine" company. Groups of factories in close proximity to each other could share resources—good business sense.

One ghost hunter that recently visited the glue factory located on the outskirts of Milwaukee said it was even more massive and depressing than she'd imagined. "There are big pits there that must have held mixers. There are even some old beaters there." She goes on to say that if you want to see the old equipment and you can't find your way into the building through a door, you can find several ways into the building through the roof.

The factory, in addition to being a ghost hunter's dream, is also an important historical site. The young lady ghost hunter said she ran into a man in his early 30s who was checking out old architecture in the Oak Creek/South Milwaukee area. He said he was curious to see if his photos would capture orbs, even though that wasn't his main purpose in visiting sites like the glue factory. His friend recently visited the factory at night and every one of his photos contained smoky streaks and orbs. The man said that while he didn't particularly believe in ghosts, there was something about being in the factory, especially in the beaters area, that was extremely unsettling.

The factory is often described as "creepy" and "dangerous" even though no one ever seems to tell trespassers to leave the premises. One visitor said there's plenty of evidence that many others frequent the factory.

Do ghosts glide through the broken panes in the swinging doors inside the factory? Some say they get a strange feeling when they look at the support pillars, like someone or something is on the other side, watching them pass by.

One can imagine the old metal carts with ancient wheels, still inside the factory, creaking along under the ghostly guiding hand of those that used to work there. How many died here while performing their jobs? How many are still here doing their jobs? The number is estimated to be in the dozens.

Paranormal investigative teams and thrill seekers alike often spend the night here. All report some kind of paranormal activity, whether it's noises and footsteps that have no source, extreme colds spots, or orbs.

The factory has closed long ago, but the ghosts of those that worked here haven't seemed to notice yet.

Warning: Heed the "No Trespassing" signs. They're there for a reason.

Chapter 35

Nashotah House

This Episcopal seminary is located in Delafield, west of Milwaukee. Founded in 1842 and chartered in 1847, it is the oldest charted institution of higher learning in Wisconsin. The area itself has been inhabited since the 1500s. Nashotah House is north of Delafield, off Highway C, hidden by towering trees.

Like all hauntingly beautiful places, Nashotah House also has its share of tragedy. The twisted story of a hanging that took place in the 1700s, as well as a woods full of ghosts that was seen by two well-respected clergy, have kept those interested in theological ghosts and ghost hunters in general, coming back time and time again.

The well-known hanging that took place on the grounds was originally believed to be suicide. The dead seminary student was buried in a cornfield as a reminder to other students that suicide is a sin. It wasn't until later that the student's wife, on her deathbed, confessed two things: she'd been having an affair with the dean, and she was responsible for her husband's death. Pretty sensational for those days.

The seminarians, wanting to set the cornfield burial right, exhumed the coffin only to find it empty.

Is the ghost reportedly seen walking the grounds the murdered seminarian? Or is it someone else? Many are buried here.

There are problems with this story; some dates don't match up as some believe they should. This doesn't necessarily mean the events didn't happen. It might just mean the events took place long ago and may not have been recorded properly—maybe on purpose to lessen the Church's responsibility for the wrongful burial of the hanged seminarian.

Regardless of when the hanging happened and the exact details, a ghostly monk has been seen walking the grounds many times in the ensuing years.

The other case, perhaps even more sensational, is about the burial, or rather the reburial, of Reverend William Lloyd Breck, one of the founders of the Nashotah Theological Seminary at Nashotah. When he died, he was originally buried in California. The Church of Wisconsin later requested that his body be exhumed and brought to Nashotah. No one could have guessed the ensuing brouhaha.

It began shortly after Breck's body arrived at the seminary. Watchers, as was customary at the time, sat with the body. Not my cup of tea, but in the days before television and the Internet, it was probably a nice break from nonstop praying and studying. In any event, on the night before the reburial, Dr. Wilson, one of the watchers, took a break from his duties and stepped outside the building. Almost immediately he rushed back inside exclaiming, "Dorset, Dorset, the woods are full of ghosts!"

Reverend Charles P. Dorset, another watcher, immediately rushed outside. What Dorset and Wilson saw could only be described as shocking. Though many dark figures darted through the woods, Wilson and Dorset couldn't get close to them. They finally returned to Breck's body, shaken. The two men had seen not one ghost, but a pack of them.

But that wasn't the end of the strange goings-on. When Breck's casket was raised the next morning, the floor beneath the casket was black. More incredible: a hole had burned through the floor. No logical or scientific explanation could be found; watchers were present throughout. Nothing untoward or unusual happened as the watchers sat with the body, certainly nothing that involved the creation of a fire.

The burial took place as planned. That night, though, as faculty was discussing the incredible events of the past few days, a loud commotion interrupted them. Dr. Gardiner, the president at the time, raced out of the room they were in, but found no one outside the door. As might be expected, the noise immediately stopped when he opened the door.

Gardiner returned to the room and sat down. The loud commotion began again. Again, he raced outside and found nothing. This time the building was searched for the source of the noise. A search turned up nothing suspicious. When the racket began a third time, Gardiner went to the hall and said, "If you are gentlemen, be still." The noises ceased. You can take this any way you like, but ghosts—most ghosts anyway—do not like to be referred to as ghosts; they tend to think of themselves as men and women.

A student took a photograph of the cemetery after the reburial of Dr. Breck. The foreground shows two graves; nothing strange about that. However, the Reverend Dr. Cole, a former president of the seminary, in full canonicals, was standing at the foot of one grave. He had been dead for some time.

Standing at the foot of the other grave is a woman who was a benefactress of the school. The grave she was standing at: her own.

Authorities explained the apparition of Reverend Dr. Cole and the benefactress as shadows caused by plant life and lighting. When they had the photographs transferred to a screen by a stereopticon, however, the figures came out so unmistakably lifelike, they could not deny the apparitions were those of the benefactress and Reverend Dr. Cole.

The student who took the pictures was being accused of creating the "ghost photograph." The student denied the accusations and went one step better to prove his innocence. He reminded the authorities that there were no photographs of Cole in existence.

Mary Sutherland.

Chapter 36
Mary Sutherland and Burlington Haunted Tours

Most of us would find all the reported paranormal activity concentrated in Burlington and the surrounding area unnerving, and maybe even a little frightening. Not Mary Sutherland, owner and operator of the Sci-Fi Café and Gift Shop, and the Earth Mysteries Museum located in downtown Burlington. She embraces it. Mary also leads the wildly popular Haunted Tours, and heads the Paranormal Research Center, as well as Paranormal BUFO Radio. Her work has been documented in newspapers like the Milwaukee Journal Sentinel, on the Web, and in books.

Mary has spent most of her life researching ancient races and underground tunnels (of which Burlington has more than its share). Incredibly, her searches have taken her and her husband, Brad, all across the United States. However, it wasn't until six years ago that they settled in the town of Burlington, whose history is steeped in mystery and violence.

Burlington's myriad mysteries holds endless fascination for this knowledgeable and passionate researcher. Is it a coincidence the museum is housed on a haunted site where bones were discovered? The Sci-Fi Café adjacent to the museum was once a speakeasy and brothel frequented by Al Capone. How many hapless, unknown victims of those violent times still haunt the building?

The Sci-Fi Café and Gift Shop not only dishes up out-of-this-world food (and has some really cool gifts), it also serves as a gathering spot for those with an interest in the paranormal.

Visitors to the café, beware: a ghost dog has been trying to untie the shoes of Sci-Fi café patrons. One customer even double-knots the strings of his shoes to make sure the dog can't untie them.

Step inside the museum and you'll instantly see how much time Mary has spent researching not just Burlington, but the world. When you listen to her explain the items in the museum, you realize she believes that Burlington is not only very haunted, but also the site of myriad mysteries that extend beyond the boundaries of what a simple haunting entails.

Inside the museum, you'll find information about the ancient history and tradition of the Native American Indians. Ancient artifacts such as a million-year-old skull, primitive stone tools, ancient crematory remains, burial idols, coins, beads, Roswell UFO artifacts, shell hammers and tools, shell net weights, prehistoric Megladon teeth, and treasure maps, are on display.

Whether you have a question about spirits, UFOs, or the symbology of the buildings and design of the city of Burlington, it's more than likely Mary can answer it for you.

The Haunted Tours, led by Mary on Saturday evenings or by appointment, are an experience you won't soon forget. Even those who don't believe in spirits or ghosts don't have the same views when they end the tour.

One large man, weighing about 300 pounds, was skeptical when he entered the woods as part of Mary's tour. Whether it was the invisible shove that nearly knocked him off his feet, or the extreme feeling of being watched, he left a very changed man.

Mary graciously shut down the Sci-Fi Café to take my daughter and I on a tour of the area, including several haunted Mormon sites, the River of Death, and the Haunted Woods Tour. My daughter and I both experienced strong feelings of being watched. The Haunted Woods crematorium area was one place especially where the hair on my arms rose and stayed that way until we were well away from the area.

Sci-Fi Café, Burlington.

During the tour, your camera might capture orbs, strange patches of light, parts of others' bodies disappearing as they shift into other dimensions.

I was literally shocked when I returned home and brought my photos up on my computer screen. Photos I took that same day in Milwaukee, Mukwonago, and in between, turned out normal; my camera is only a few months old. The photos I took in the Burlington Public Cemetery, near the River of Death, the death place of James Jesse Strang, and the location where the Strang plates were located, all showed oddities such as odd globs of white that are randomly strewn across some parts of my photos.

Most shocking of all—the photos I took during the Haunted Tour show areas of my daughter's body that are bright for no reason. Parts of other photos are blurry where they should be clear, and vice versa.

Far and away, the most incredible thing captured on one of my photos: the face of a Native American wearing what can only be described as ceremonial dress. It looks like a small blur until you double its size. Then the image is so clear it takes your breath away. Guardian trees in the forest are said to hold the spirits of long gone Native Americans who lived in the forest thousands of years ago.

Mary told me about four or five years ago that the woods started feeding off what she refers to as psychic energy. Since last year, the energy has gotten much more intense. I'm still not sure how I feel about the incredible photos I took, but I do know that when you are in those woods, you know you are in a haunted place.

To see it captured on film filled me with not only wonder, but uneasiness as well. What and who are the beings in those woods? The Haunted Tour usually takes place at night when orbs are better captured, but I took the tour during the day and I still captured all the things described above.

Crematorium, Haunted Woods.

In the Haunted Woods, don't be surprised if your camera acts up or the batteries go dead unexpectedly.

One man who took the Haunted Tour saw a young girl dressed in an 1800s outfit. Astonished, he turned to tell his wife what he was seeing. When they turned back, the girl had vanished.

Another woman who took the tour saw a white fence, just as clear as can be, that disappeared a moment later.

The sounds of people talking who aren't there is another common occurrence. You might hear whispering in your ear when no one is around. A strong sense of imminent danger may overwhelm you along the way.

There are some who take the Haunted Tour that vow never again to enter the woods once they are safely away. The Haunted Woods is a mysterious beautiful place. It isn't hard to imagine spirits so thick they have to compete for space in the dense foliage.

We'll never know how many humans died in the woods, but it's a safe guess the crematorium is likely responsible for the disposal of countless human bodies throughout the ages. The charred rocks are testament to times that happened long ago.

Collapsed earth, covered with stones, mark the places of ancient dwellings. Many undoubtedly died in those places, too.

Nikki Linzmeier on the Haunted Tour. Strange bleaching on her legs. No flash used, overcast day.

Also unnerving is a place on the tour where you are unable to stand up after turning around in a circle.

One of the most convincing aspects that the woods really are haunted are the sheer number of orbs and other inexplicable things captured on film.

If you're thinking that film can easily be doctored—you're right. It can be, but not in this case. Once the tour is finished, all members return to the Sci-Fi Café to immediately download their cameras into a computer. The images are immediately shown on screen. Even if you think someone else may have tinkered with their results, your camera will tell the story for you. Not everyone captures something, but many do.

This is one experience you truly have to experience for yourself. And while you're here, take in the incredible number of other haunted hotspots in town.

Mary Sutherland will be happy to guide you to a better understanding of all that is paranormal in Burlington. Learn more about the ghosts of Burlington by paying a visit to the Sci-Fi Café and Gift Shop, Paranormal BUFO Internet Radio, Earth Mysteries Museum, Haunted Tours, and Paranormal Research Center, located at 532 N. Pine Street in downtown Burlington. Or give Mary a call at 212-767-1116.

Chapter 37

Haunted Burlington

To look at this quaint city southwest of Milwaukee, you would never guess it is called a ghost hunter's dream, an orb photographer's dream, and an ancient mysteries researcher's dream.

You might never guess it was built on top of ancient burial grounds, just like the town in the movie, *Poltergeist*. In fact, the town is believed to be built on twenty-seven different mounds! This charming town known to many as Chocolate City, USA, the home of Nestlé candy bars, just may be the home of the most concentrated paranormal activity anywhere.

Skeletal Remains

Excavation to lay foundations for several downtown buildings in Burlington unearthed numerous human bones. Skeletal remains were found under the Top Museum, Risso & Diersen, S.C., and Kreins Color Barn, on North Pine Street. A walk past these businesses, even in the daytime, gives you the feeling that you are being watched.

Malt House Theater

The Malt House Theater, home of the Haylofters Community Theater, even has their own ghost they call "Esmeralda." She's been seen floating in an area behind the theater, wearing a long blue dress. The Malt House Theater is located at 109 N. Main Street.

Even newer buildings, like the Kmart on Highway 36 on the outskirts of town, aren't immune to paranormal activity. Kmart was the site of some very dramatic poltergeist-like activity in March of 2000.

Employees working the night shift said toys began falling off shelves and then rolling down the aisles. In addition to the phone ringing for no reason, someone or something apparently had the munchies that night. The clean sandwich grill began cooking imaginary hot dogs. The smell was delicious. The thought of ghosts making snacks was a little disconcerting.

Phones in the building were checked and no mechanical problems were detected. Police dogs were even brought in to look for intruders, but none were found.

Some employees at the store say they've never had a paranormal encounter of any kind at the store. Others have a different story. One employee who wished to remain anonymous said, "Sometimes I get this weird feeling someone is watching me—like really close, but when you turn around there's no one there. It's really creepy."

Haunted Oak

Kellie, a regular at the Sci-Fi Café in downtown Burlington, believes the huge oak tree on Highway 11, a short distance from downtown, is haunted. In the early 1960s, a man killed his girlfriend and threw her over the bridge near the oak tree. About ten years ago, a man leading the police on a high speed chase crashed into the tree and was pronounced dead at the scene. Then, in early 2006, a man on a motorcycle was pulling away from a nearby home. He was struck by a pickup truck and left for dead. The man in the pickup truck drove to Bray Road and shot himself after a standoff with the police. This chain of events began near the same oak tree.

Ghostly Encounters

Ghosts are literally everywhere in Burlington, along with associated paranormal activity. Human bones have also been found on the old fairgrounds. Ghostly encounters happen regularly, as do reports of portals to dimensional worlds opening and closing.

Ancient Tunnel System

Sound incredible? Not to those who know Burlington's secrets. There's an ancient tunnel system running under the surface of town. Luckily, most of the entrances have been sealed off. But who can be sure if there aren't more tunnel entrances waiting to be discovered? Beasts similar to the Bray Road Beast are rumored to live in the tunnels. Mary Sutherland took me to a well-known spot where a beast was seen and said to have killed numerous farm animals.

Voree

As mentioned before, Burlington is associated with another name—Voree—known intimately by the Mormon community. Voree is often referred to as the Promised Land or the "New Jerusalem." Prophet James J. Strang discovered three metal plates buried in a hillside under the roots of a giant tree. This special place is just a short distance off Mormon Road, deep in the woods. An impressive marker notes the spot that few will ever see. A feeling of oppressiveness, and maybe fear and anger, accompanies it.

Symbology

Anyone who studies ancient knowledge knows Burlington is alive in the occult and symbology. The Mormon name "Mormo" translates into "King of the Ghouls" or the living dead. The buildings on Pine Street and Chestnut Street hold myriad symbols.

Who is responsible for these symbols? The unnamed founders of the town? Former Mormon settlers? Someone else? Whoever it is, the symbols were decided on long, long ago.

River of Death

The White River in Burlington is known as the River of the Dead. Mormons were said to baptize on behalf of the dead. These proxy baptisms involved living Mormons temporarily assuming the names of dead people.

The cemeteries in Burlington have been called the most haunted in the state. The Burlington Public Cemetery is included in numerous Web sites as haunted. Photos taken at night especially show phantom lights, orbs, and other anomalies.

White River, also known as the River of Death.

A smaller cemetery known as Potters Field is one of the most famous, or perhaps infamous, cemeteries in Wisconsin. Located on Brown Lake Road, the cemetery is said to lie on an ancient burial ground. People that have visited the cemetery said they were chased away by something they can't see, but feel very strongly. They feel as if they are being pushed away.

You can learn more about Burlington on the Web at: burlintonwisconsinmysteries.com and burlingtonwi.com.

Unique marker in the Burlington Public Cemetery.

Chapter 38

Victoria and Anna

Shirley and her grandmother, Anna, have a special bond that transcends even death.

Anna was born in Prussia in 1842, but wasn't old-fashioned like most other grandmothers Shirley knew. Anna believed anyone should be able to follow their dreams—including women. She painted when she wasn't caring for her family or helping with chores on the family farm in Cedarburg. She spoke fluent English, German, and Polish, and encouraged her children and grandchildren to learn languages. She learned Native American herbal remedies and customs from one of the few Native American families in the area, along with some of their greetings and phrases so she could converse with them in their native tongue if she met them on the street.

What Shirley remembers most, however, is that her grandmother's love of language went past the usual borders. Anna talked to the dead. A lot.

Shirley remembers staying with grandmother one summer when she was about eleven or twelve.

"I was going to surprise her by buying some licorice for her," Shirley remembers. "Grandma Anna loved licorice, but never bought any for herself."

Shirley put her nickel and pennies in her pocket and started off toward the country store.

"I walked for what seemed like forever, but was probably only about fifteen minutes or so. Suddenly I had this strange feeling come over me—like someone was leading me by the hand to the side of the road."

Shirley said she wasn't tired, yet she could barely move one foot in front of the other. She sat down under a tree and promptly fell asleep. The long tall grass hid her and also made a very comfortable bed. The next thing she knew, her grandmother was shaking her awake.

Disoriented, Shirley sat up and looked around. "Grandma began scolding me in Polish. She always used Polish when she was upset. Then she asked me if I was all right."

When Shirley assured her grandmother that she was fine, Anna reminded Shirley that money was hard to come by, and buying licorice for an old lady was a waste of money.

Shirley was shocked. "How did you know I was going to buy you licorice?" she asked.

"Victoria told me."

It was all Shirley could do not to roll her eyes.

Victoria was Anna's sister; she died of a fever when she was seventeen, and was said to have been the most beautiful girl in all of Königsberg.

"Victoria said you're lucky you stopped when you did. There's a big snake a little ways up the road, and you're too young to die like she did."

Shirley remembers crying after hearing her grandmother's words. She can't remember if she cried because she could have been bitten by a snake, or because a ghost was keeping tabs on her every move.

"After you didn't answer my calls, I started walking to the pond, but Victoria told me you were on your way to the store and there was good chance you'd be bitten by a snake. She said she'd try to stall you. Good thing she did."

Shirley, though young, was skeptical. She got to her feet and glanced up the road. "I don't see any snake." They both left the ditch and went to the front of the truck.

Shirley remembers looking back at where she had been resting. The spot was hidden by tall, dense grasses. How had her grandmother spotted her?

"You must have been looking for me for a long time," Shirley told her grandmother, feeling ashamed she had made the old woman leave the house to search for her.

"No," Grandma Anna replied. "Victoria told me exactly where to find you. She said she brought you here."

Shirley gasped. That was the exact feeling she had experienced—someone leading her away from the road.

"Since we're halfway there, we might as well go to the store. I need flour anyway. You can pick something out for yourself if you wish."

Shirley and her grandmother got in the old truck and started up the road. About a half mile later, Anna stopped the truck. A big brown snake was loosely coiled in the middle of the road, sunning itself.

"Thank you, Victoria," Anna said as if talking to someone right in front of her, and then drove around the snake to the store.

Shirley can't remember if the snake was a rattlesnake or a pine snake. All she can remember is feeling so weak in the knees that she could barely get out of the truck when they finally reached the store.

Through the years, Anna had a number of messages for Shirley from Victoria. They all proved to be true and involved things Shirley had done that no one else besides her knew. Slowly but surely, Shirley became a believer in ghosts.

Anna was healthy of mind and body well into her nineties. When Shirley came to pay Anna what would be her last earthly visit, Anna was living in an apartment on the outskirts of Milwaukee. The first thing out of Grandma Anna's mouth was, "Victoria came by to see me this morning."

Shirley prepared herself for some amusing anecdote. Instead, Anna said, "I'll be going home tomorrow."

Anna appeared in good health; she had color in her cheek and hadn't been ill. She still played cards with a couple of the elderly neighbors every week.

"Tell her she's going to have to wait. I'm not ready to let you go," Shirley teased, though her heart was heavy.

"I'm ready, dear," Anna told her with a gentle smile. She changed the subject and they later ate a meal at a downtown restaurant. As Shirley dropped her off, Anna said, "When I'm gone, all you have to do is call for me if you need me. Just like I do with Victoria."

Shirley smiled. Her grandmother's belief in ghosts was stronger than ever. Shirley kissed her goodbye.

The next day, Shirley called her grandmother, but there was no answer. She and her mother quickly went to Anna's apartment. Just as Anna said, she had gone to join Victoria. Anna's body lay on her sofa. She was dressed in a nice pantsuit and her rosary, from the old country, was wound around her hands, which were folded in prayer.

Shirley says she thinks of her grandmother often and feels her presence: protective, soothing, and happy, just like when her grandmother was alive.

"I've talked to her many times," she says. "I may not see her, but I hear her voice."

An Interview with Noah Voss

Founder of
GetGhostGear.com Enterprises

Noah Voss, founder GetGhostGear.com Enterprises. *Courtesy of Noah Voss.*

Noah keeps busy running his three websites; GetGhostGear.com, where he has been selling paranormal investigating equipment worldwide since 2000; UFOwisconsin.com, where he regularly posts new reports on Wisconsin's UFO phenomena; and W-Files.com, which has been featuring all things odd, since it was first published in 1997. He has worked with such companies as the History Channel, Triage Entertainment, and Lions Gate Films on projects ranging from UFO documentaries to ABC's Scariest Places on Earth.

Noah has also appeared in print and on international radio programs broadcasted in over forty countries, such as Wake Up America, A UFO Study, The Kevin Smith Show, and Wisconsin's very own, Unexplained Radio Show.

Recently, Noah and I had a Q&A session to learn more about him and what he does.

Q: First of all, can you tell me about GetGhostGear.com?

A: *I'd love to, Sherry! GetGhostGear.com is an online paranormal investigating equipment superstore. Visitors can view and purchase equipment that has been collected into one convenient website, supplying the paranormal researcher and investigator. The idea for the site came about while I began to notice an entire industry that was not having its wants and needs catered to. It was the year 2000 and I had already been researching and investigating the mysterious and unknown for over a decade to one extent or another. I saw a need in the paranormal industry for many resources and actual tools that could be made better available for those persons in the industry .I had a vision of the paranormal sphere becoming further respected and better understood. I felt in order for that to happen, people needed a resource just like what www.GetGhostGear. com has become...*

In the early years, [people] were applying the oldest and most traditional investigative methods, such as your own senses and tools we still offer like dowsing rods. Along with tradition investigative tools, we currently offer the newest, most cutting edge, scientific technology—for instance, night vision goggles and thermal infrared imaging...People had to search out other very specific scientific fields and apply a high level of understanding in the scientific principles in order to find, acquire, and then properly attain readings from their new equipment. Not only that, but also teach themselves how to interpret the data correctly. At the time, the best you could hope for was an established author in the field who offered only several pieces of paranormal equipment. Often, through no fault of their own, these authors had few other resources to offer the budding investigator...

...One of our most popular resource centers is our "World Environment" page. With the power of the Internet, we are able to put together in one comprehensive location, a "Solar X Ray" and "Geomagnetic Field" monitor that is nearly instantaneously updated and explained in detail,

along with current local weather and searchable weather databases, "Moon Phases" reviewable past and present, real time "Seismic" and "Volcanic" global mapping, as well as links to "Biological Fronts", including water table levels, pollutions, such as national acid rain maps—all portent information to your specific investigation area, no matter where your location.

GetGhostGear.com in its entirety is around 100 pages in size, full of "Knowledge Centers" where a visitor can learn about the equipment sold, as well as a members' area and "Resource Centers" where the subject matter is further broken down by interest.

Q: What are some of the reasons people contact you?

A: *That seems to have changed even the short time I have been in the industry. I suppose there are as many unique answers to that question as there have been specific people who chose to contact my organization. Approximately half my cases would come through a group I founded in the 1990s with several other researchers. We called it P.I.R.O. or the Paranormal Investigating Researchers Organization. P.I.R.O. served me well in its time. However, I have since moved away from utilizing limited resources to support an organization and now focus on individual research through industry contacts.*

The more common issue in the past would have been people contacting me out of fear. The persons involved would be encountering an unknown situation that they had, in most cases, turned to all the usual channels for help and found none fully capable of finding a resolution. Fear of the unknown is not a new or uncommon trait, and people were looking to us in hopes that we might rule out some possibilities, while shedding some new light on their unique experiences. People would be hesitant to categorize or name what they were experiencing. Instead they would just share odd situations such as unexplainable noises like knocking, footsteps when home alone, doors opening, and seeing wisps of shadows move about.

With the paranormal industry currently going through another flux in the public's eye via the onslaught of television shows and related spin-offs, people now seem to contact us more often with industry lingo. Some feel they had experiences that unequivocally prove a paranormal happening, such as orbs or shadow people, even possessions and physical attacks.

I and my associates have decades of experience to fall back on. However, with limited resources, we sometimes are not able to best assist any one particular situation. In those cases, we advise people to use tried and trusted support networks first, whether that is a friend, family, teacher, counselor, religious peer, or even in some cases, the police. We never sell ourselves as the end-all be-all answer to everyone's problems. I and my associates help who we can, where we can, and as much as we can. More often than not, people contact us because they have nowhere else to turn.

Q: What type of equipment do you need to safely confirm your suspicions about a ghostly entity?

A: *This is a question I receive often, and one I usually feel requires qualifying my response. To answer your question as straight away as possible, every case is unique and requires situational-specific equipment and knowledge. We intelligently approach the experience being reported through a combination of scientific principle—even with all its faults—and logical reasoning.*

I guess another way to answer your question would be confirmation not dependant on equipment alone, but rather objective logical approach of the investigation. I suppose you could say the approach is the equipment as much as the gadgets being held. Having an open minded, objective perspective while observing the situation and people having the experiences, is crucial to quantifying experiences with equipment. This further requires a discipline of not jumping to unfounded or unconnected conclusions, but rather of stepping off one known or accepted fact to another, until a logical and verifiable (as possible) conclusion can be reached. This may lead you to acquiring additional data not first collected due to a new perspective gained during your initial investigation or review of the data acquired. This then might require a second investigation, this one then utilizing new equipment specifically suited to the new theory, hopefully uncovering additional data that helps to support or disprove your theory.

While "suspicions" may be right on, the assumed fact that we in the industry know what a 'ghostly entity' is, or that one even exists in the sense that we as a general society perceive them to be, is quite uncertain. Now I know this may be an unpopular stance for some, but let me expand. It is perfectly acceptable in our world today, while utilizing a faith-based, mythos-belief system to subjectively come to conclusions based on experiences had in a non-quantified manner. It should, in my opinion, be included in any one person or organization's statements of findings or conclusions of paranormal investigations.

Again, while that is a perfectly acceptable stance in the world today, and those taking that approach to the paranormal field are in no way better or worse, I simply strive for a different approach as a whole. Accepting the fact that there is no proven 'ghost detector', we can look at some suggestions I have based on hundreds, if not thousands, of paranormal cases I have worked on. In any one investigation there seems to me, a nearly insurmountable number of variables to monitor, control, or explain. For instance, in an imaginary case where a Milwaukee resident is reporting chills and cold spots in their home, they continually but sporadically see shadows move about out of the corners of their eyes, and even awake at night unable to catch their breath. The last straw for them was finding orbs in their daughter's thirteenth birthday pictures.

Let's approach this, not with a debunker's perspective, but one of healthy skepticism so we may objectively attempt to find some possibilities for what the family is experiencing. Possibilities, with the chills and cold spots being reported, could be a malfunctioning microwave, short circuit in the home's electrical system, or even an outdated and overloaded power junction box hidden in the walls. All of these possibilities can be measured, tested, and quantifiably measured, and recorded... These few, out of many mundane possibilities, in my opinion, should be ruled out. If they are not found to be the cause of the chills and cold spots, then we are slightly closer to being able to speculate on less known phenomena, such as a ghostly presence.

The same can be done with the report of shadows moving about out of the corners of the witness' eyes. Optometrists could administer eye tests and question the witness to facilitate in removing potential explanations, as well as catching any health issues that may be affecting the witness' sight. Video camera systems would be ideal for monitoring the reported locations of shadows, as well as kenneling any pets, and sending any children to stay the night at a friend's home.

We are not proving or disproving with any of these approaches, simply minimizing the possibility of commonplace causes for the experiences being reported. What about a witness being unable to catch their breath while awaking from sleep? I myself suffer from sleep apnea, and have similar experiences almost nightly. This again can be diagnosed or ruled out by a medical doctor. As for the orbs, first I would examine the camera(s) in question and see if there were any physical explanations such as a dirty lens, or a malfunction in the electronics. Ruling this out, an attempt should be made to recreate the orbs in a controlled situation, where there may be pet dander, dust, or other air particulates about that would be identical to the earlier orbs captured. Were the orbs in question taken when the furnace was on or central air conditioning running? The added air movement of that or a window being open could add to the potential variables. However, if there is a ghost present, who is to say that they do not appear exactly the same as a speck of dust in the sunlight?

Q: What three ghost "hunting" items do you think are indispensable?

A: My choice of items—or for that matter, your choice as the reader—depends exclusively on what you hope to gain from your investigations and your specific belief system. Those who are in it for the adventure might choose their favorite beverage; those of a religious background may opt for a beloved holy item for protection. As for me, if we consider the human perception capability as one of our three "ghost hunting items", this is the most indispensable. Whether using the accepted forms of biological input; touch, sight, smell, and sound, or considering yourself open to information gained via extra sensory perception, be mindful of it.

Not gone are the days where sensitives moved about an area sharing their impressions of the unseen and mostly unverifiable ethereal. These are all still valid parts of an investigation until proven otherwise, and something can be learned from utilizing all methods. In my opinion, it should of course, be backed up by external quantitative data whenever possible. For that I like tools or paranormal investigating equipment that pull double duty, or for that matter quadruple duty... [like equipment that] is capable of monitoring temperature, humidity, wind speed, and light levels [and much more]... [See the GetGhost website for other equipment details.]

This is an important step forward in paranormal research as it allows the investigator to further study the data acquired, looking for trends or anomalies that could not be otherwise explained. Since you can't necessarily not take yourself on a paranormal investigation, I would have to add a micro cassette recorder to make my list three. This isn't solely for the acquisition of EVP's (use an external microphone please) or electronic voice phenomena, but rather for keeping a clear and objective record of the investigation, should you encounter a situation worthy of notating. I consider my own mind and memory as fallible as everyone else's, and an audible recording of events can allow the most subtle and otherwise forgotten observations to be kept for later analysis. Above all, make sure you take your scientific, open minded, and safety conscious self into the field, and you should always come away with something beneficial.

Q: What would you consider a positive indicator or indication of a ghostly encounter?

A: *I like that "positive indicator" as opposed to proof. I think, as you so eloquently worded your question around, that they are two entirely different things. Indisputable proof positive of a ghost being, spirit, spook, or specter is not currently available in my opinion. There is substantial data showing great unknowns in our western science. With that thought in the very forefront of our minds, we can move forward with the question. Let's look at the same example as before of a Milwaukee resident's haunting, this time without poor ventilation, malfunctioning appliances, bad electrical wiring, or even sleep apnea.*

Suppose for a moment that we had unlimited resources on our investigation and completely exhausted all other known possibilities. A positive indicator for a ghostly encounter might be the presence of questions or unexplainable readings in our data when all other known possibilities have been removed from the greater realm of likelihood. What we are left with then is a truly anomalous phenomena or an indicator of something else, possibly a ghostly encounter should there be other substantial facts indicative of that. It is difficult to say in a black and white, non e-prime manner for me. A ghostly encounter, being such a subjective experience, only adds to my quandary. For some it is enough to have small orbs develop in their pictures that were not seen at the time it was taken. For me that is too large of a jump from a known fact to a finite conclusion.

Another way to look at the complexity of the question is what makes a ghost? A ghost's reality has not been completely accepted by the world we live in or the sciences that currently dictate it. So how could we in the end, clearly and to reach enough people with their varying ideas of what a ghost is, conclude an indication of a ghostly encounter? I suppose for me, it might take the classic visually full-bodied apparition, intelligently communicating with me, enough provable information to repeat or at least convince my peers in the industry of my experience.

At this point of my research and investigation, it commonly comes down to probability. What is the most likely, perhaps statistically speaking, reason for any particular outcome? Of course if we look at the data acquired and attempt to form mathematical formulas showing probability, then we run into similar issues Dr. Drake ran into with the Drake Equation. Looking to figure out how many planets in our universe could potentially hold life, forces one to speculate and hypothesize on information that still lies in the greater unknown. Ghosts in the paranormal field still posses this similar issue of unknowns.

Q: What prompted your lifelong passion of the paranormal?

A: *I've always had a strong interest in mysteries and the unknown. Starting as a very young child, I was of the persuasion to always ask "Why?", so I'm told. Through elementary school* when one begins book reports, I consistently read about UFO's, ghosts, Bigfoot, and so on. My love for the paranormal only grew from there. I continued reading and absorbing all and any related material I could find. Somewhere along the line I reached a point in my research where I wasn't getting the answers. That brought about my taking the visits I made to the locations I learned about further. I recall taking EVPs with a full-sized tape recorder at my friend's house because of its purported haunting. I was at the ripe old age of eight or so.

Looking to acquire my own data and form my own educated positions on the matter, I started seeking out more advanced equipment. I did this for years, until I became further involved in the industry. I wanted to learn from people who had been practicing this interest longer. I attended lectures and conferences for many years, in a number of states. I eventually became aware of the need for someone to outfit the paranormal investigator because it took me so long and so many resources to find and acquire the equipment I needed. I met other people in my same situation and figured there must be newcomers to the industry that could benefit from our work. I was motivated to establishing business contacts and tools to help move the paranormal 'sciences' forward beyond what I could do on my own.

Later, I began www.GetGhostGear.com. Since then, I've had the opportunity to further my interests and passions in other fields: running multiple websites, lecturing at conferences and colleges across the entire upper Midwest, along with publishing my first book, UFO Wisconsin, in 2007. My experiences along the way have been a wonderful adventure full of opportunity, not only to visit new places, but interact with people I would have never otherwise had the chance to meet. I've learned so many things from my travels that it is both tragic and motivating to me how much more there is to learn.

Q: Have you had an experience in the Milwaukee area that still makes you shake your head, or has you thanking your lucky stars you escaped unscathed?

A: It has been my experience that on most any investigation into the unknown, it is not the ghosts that need be worried about, but rather the living. While on an excursion searching for the ghost town of Ulao, we were sent the hottest day of the year. Humid and indexes of over 100 degrees made the climbs up and down the cliffs along Lake Michigan an added challenge. We had ultra lights and airplanes buzz only a stone's throw above us and plenty of bugs. It all added to the adventure and made finding the old remains all the more gratifying. Nothing too horribly frightening to report, I'm afraid—or rather not afraid. There are some in the industry that joke the safest place to be in a haunted house is with a paranormal investigator because they never experience the ghosts.

Q: What's new or cutting edge in the world of paranormal detection?

A: A great question! On a lot of fronts, not much has changed since Charles Fort or Harry Price investigated unusual mysteries a long lifetime ago. The dynamic of the paranormal field hasn't allowed for any large industry-wide leaps forward in thinking or agreed facts. Moving from a time when metaphysical ruled, dowsing rods, crystals, and sensitives were just some tools of the trade. The technology has noticeably evolved in the last one hundred years. We've come from a day when using a magnetic compass and early cameras were the cutting edge, to electronic equipment monitoring nearly every known aspect of our environment.

One of the not so new, but certainly cost prohibitive pieces of equipment, would be thermal imaging technology. Utilized by the military and fire fighting operations alike, it could be described as a video camera that allows the user to monitor normally unseen radiation wave lengths that register in the form of heat signatures. The theory here is that perhaps some of the anomalous phenomena being experienced may be related to ghosts or forces that are not detectable with our unaided eye. Currently you should be ready to spend around $12,000 for a new, color introduction level unit. Significantly less expensive starting around $200 are night vision goggles... I do like the multipurpose function of this investment for your investigation bag. By magnifying the available or artificially enhanced light, you are able to see in complete darkness. Using a monoscope harness version of these keeps your hands free, weight down, and your exploring near limitless. There are attachments that allow you to connect these to your video or still frame cameras, providing another huge insight on your investigations. Adding another lens or infrared illuminator allows the cryptozoologist or UFOlogist the added benefit of monitoring things in the dark from distances of over 300 yards. Those lengths are ideal for stalking werewolves, the elusive Martian, or that abandoned, run-down, spooky house at the end of the street you are afraid to get too close to. Both of these basic technologies have been around for some time. They continually become more economical and further functioned as technology advances.

Something that is quickly becoming common place is the interfacing of the scientific equipment ... to computers. This is a very welcomed feature that will save countless hours of video recording equipment to aid in preserving a reading. This will undoubtedly create large data pools that will then need to be sifted through, looking for trends and other anomalous results in the readings. If specific and agreed upon controls can be eventually put into place, this may be an area of great interest to paranormal researchers in the future.

There are a couple other things that I have been watching for some time with great interest. I really like the lens adaptors that allow for photographs to be taken showing a full 360 degree picture of the area. If production ever increases enough to bring the price down, this could be immeasurably helpful in studying pictures claiming to hold an anomalous phenomena.

Another visual recording piece of equipment I will be awaiting with great anticipation is the holographic developers. Imagine looking at a three dimensional image of a purported ghost. The additional insight that may be gained from this technology could be very exciting.

For the most part, I feel that we as a society will need to have great advances in our understanding of simply everything around us before being able to apply detection equipment and expect anything remotely close to incontrovertible evidence. For this, I currently look to the leading minds in the world of astrophysics.

Q: What kinds of people contact you?

A: *All kinds. Quite literally, it is an extremely diverse demographic—a cross section of people from Milwaukee, Wisconsin, and indeed around the world. Through my different endeavors into the paranormal, I've had dealings with persons on nearly every continent around the globe. A bit closer to home, here in Wisconsin, it seems everyone I meet has a ghost story or unusual experience to share. The only other common trait that these people share is that they usually don't like to let on that they have this experience to tell me, until I'm alone.*

Q: Do you have a "dream" ghost or location you would like to investigate someday?

A: *Too many to name. I have put a lot of my resources into traveling so far in my life. I take great pleasure in seeing new places and learning about different cultures. Thus far I've had the good fortune to travel to all but about four states here in America. I've researched ghostly St. Augustine, Florida, investigated the mysterious Winchester Mansion in California, UFOs in Mexico, haunted highways in Hawaii, voodoo in Jamaica, and searched for Sasquatch in British Columbia. I would love to return to Mexico and spend more time with the ancient civilization remnants and the infamous 'dead zone'. I hope to visit Great Britain sooner than later; tour as many castles, catacombs, and pubs as possible, and probably should do so in that order. I have Swiss and German heritage and would enjoy very much learning firsthand about their societal relationship with topics such as the paranormal.*

Q: Why do you believe ghosts interact with the world of the living?

A: *When one starts discussing beliefs, to me they have come to the point where faith has played at least some function. Not discussing faith as a religion; but rather confidence in the face of uncertainty, trust in something not complete, reliance that is in part blind, or conviction that is closed to discussion or at least debate. In all honesty, I feel that what has been put forth by paranormal researchers and investigators, is as of yet, incomplete. I strive to not be of any one belief, rather open to potentials and possibilities.*

Q: Are the ghosts we see on TV and at the theater an accurate portrayal of ghosts people encounter on a daily basis?

A: *In all fairness, I suppose I can't answer that with any great certainty. In my experience, thus far, no. For the most part, movie and television portrayals of ghosts are much dramatized. While they may have some basis in fact or at least witness testimony, my experiences fall short of those seen on screen. To be fair and logical on my very fluid stance, when performing an investigation into the unknown, we are only present for a limited time. What we hope to accomplish by the means of one night, may have been experienced by the witnesses for a lifetime. Just because we as paranormal investigators do not experience what was reported to us in our brief time on site can in no way rule out that the phenomena didn't ever happen or that it won't happen after we are gone.*

Q: What do you do for fun?

A: *Ah, yes, fun; I remember it well. As with most all people these days, I find myself continually scheduled for more hours than there are in the day. My endeavors surrounding the paranormal keep me quite busy most of the time. Thankfully, I love to learn and enjoy all my time spent working in the paranormal fields. I have been told that I am not easily pigeonholed, however. I hold a college degree in Culinary Arts and still enjoy cooking whenever the time is made. Spending as many moments with my wife, Jennifer, friends, and family, are of course taken advantage of whenever possible. I enjoy harvesting vegetables from my home garden, paintball with the guys, wilderness camping, and sampling new beer; sometimes more than several. I used to make more time for snowboarding, inline skating, mountaineering, rock-climbing, hot air ballooning, and backpacking, but they seem to have slipped down my ever evolving to-do list for now. I can, and have spent entire days at the State Historical Society, local library, or book store, and am sure to do so again in the future. Should I get the occasional chance to relax, my wife and I might be found taking in a movie or sitting at home watching the X-Files or latest independent film find.*

Q: How does the ghost population of Milwaukee compare with the rest of the nation?

A: *I like pointed questions, and in all fairness this is one that paranormal researchers should have more data compiled on by now. Unfortunately, there just isn't the proper information available to intellectually comment. This does draw into sharp focus the state of the paranormal field as a science. We have a long way to go before proper archives and databases are set up and accepted by the industry. The method of acquiring statistical data must conform to agreed upon procedures. This is, in part, the issue. How does one categorize the statistical data being gathered? How does one define 'ghost' or 'haunting' for the study, and who makes the final decision? In my opinion, Milwaukee had older established communities along the coast, and Native American settlements further inland. These types of variables tend to give rise to legends, and almost set the scene for people to have ghostly experiences. The simple fact in our current society is the longer people have lived in an area, the more ghost type reports are generated.*

Of Ghostly Interest

Want to know more about ghosts?

Who doesn't? That's why I've created a list of the living, who just happen to know a lot about the no-longer living. This includes where ghosts are likely to be found, how to find them, and what to do when you find them.

Some of my favorites are listed below (in no particular order). There are many, many more not listed. Dig around. You'll be amazed at all the good stuff you'll uncover.

Some investigate the paranormal, write about it, hold tours, and sell ghost gear. Others are forums, sources of information, and just plain cool places to learn more about ghosts:

Milwaukee Area Paranormal Investigations, or M.A.P.I. Visit them on the Web at: http://www.milwaukeeparanormal.com. E-mail them for more information at: mapi@milwaukeeparanormal.com.

Southern Wisconsin Paranormal Research Group (S.W.P.R.G.) based out of Janesville, http://www.paranormalresearchgroup.homestead.com/. Check out their movie.

Wisconsin Paranormal Scientific Investigations, based located in southern Wisconsin, http://www.geocities.com/wipsi2000/index.html.

Kindred Spirits Paranormal is a non-profit paranormal research group, http://kindredspiritsparanormal.net/index.html.

Learn more about Burlington and all its mysteries by contacting Mary Sutherland, researcher, author, and owner/operator of the Sci-Fi Café and Gift Shop, Paranormal BUFO Radio, Earth Mysteries Museum, Haunted Tours, and the Paranormal Research Center, all located at 532 N. Pine Street. Phone 262-767-1116 for more information. Or visit the Web: burlintonwisconsinmysteries.com and burlingtonwi.com.

James Andrew Aho is a Milwaukee-based paranormal researcher and author. Visit: EARS: Evidence of Alien contact Revealed in Scripture, http://www.thelightside.org/ears to learn more. James is also the original founder of The W Files, an archive of Wisconsin paranormal activity.

Noah Voss, founder of GetGhostGear.com Enterprises. Visit http://www.GetGhostGear.com, http://www.UFOwisconsin.com, and http://www.w-files.com/ to learn more about paranormal investigative equipment and supplies—all that is paranormal in Wisconsin.

Milwaukee Madness 2U, is an online discussion group devoted to sharing information about haunted places, ghosts, and anything that is strange in and around Milwaukee. John Scherf is the owner/moderator. To learn more, visit: http://groups.yahoo.com:80/group/milwaukeemadness2u/.

The Shadowlands, Haunted Places in Wisconsin. The Web site provides a list and description of haunted places in Wisconsin: http://www.theshadowlands.net/places/wisconsin.htm.

View a list of haunted places in Wisconsin at: http://www.angelfire.com/psy/sewgr/hauntedwi.html.

Haunted America Tours.com. This site features information on ghosts, hauntings, and stories of the unexplained. Featured is "The Top Ten Most Haunted Cemetery or Graveyards." http://www.hauntedamericatours.com/hauntedcemeteries/toptenhauntedcemeteries/.

A list of Wisconsin's Haunted locations can be found at Haunted Wisconsin's Database: http://www.hauntedwi.com/WIXhauntedlocations.htm.

Haunted Wisconsin, Ghosts of the Prairie Web site: http://www.prairieghosts.com/hauntwi.html.

Greater Milwaukee Paranormal Research Group. Web site: http://www.gmprg-wi.com/. You'll find a wealth of fascinating information here.

Haunted Times Magazine is the magazine for those with an appetite for the paranormal: http://www.hauntedtimes.com/.

Have fun!

Selected Bibliography

BOOKS AND PERIODICALS

Balousek, Marv. 101 Wisconsin Unsolved Mysteries.Oregon, Wisconsin: Badger Books Inc., 2000.

Curtis, W.A. "Project Canterbury, Some Wisconsin Ghosts," The New York Times, December 7, 1902.

Edwards, Frank. Strange People. New York: Signet, 1961.

Endthoff, Gertrude Moe. South Milwaukee - Then To Now. South Milwaukee, Wisconsin: Journal Printing Company, 1976.

Godfrey, Linda S. and Hendricks, Richard D. Weird Wisconsin. New York: Sterling Publishing Co., Inc., 2005.

Guiley, Rosemary Ellen. The Encyclopedia of Ghosts and Spirits (second edition). New York: Checkmark Books, An imprint of Facts on File, Inc., 1982.

Norman, Michael and Scott, Beth. Haunted Heartland.

New York: Warner Books, 1985.

Stark, William F. Ghost Towns of Wisconsin. Sheboygan, Wisconsin: Zimmermann Press, 1977.

Stingl, Jim. "Pilgrimage to 'witch's house' was a rite of passage," The Milwaukee Journal Sentinel, January 11, 2002.

WEB SITES

clipclip, Research Milwaukee Ghost, http://www.clipclip.org/activity/view/246/research-milwaukee-ghosts

Ghosts of the Prairie, Haunted Wisconsin, http://www.prairieghosts.com/hauntwi.html

Haunted America Tours.com. Information on Ghost, Hauntings and Stories of the Unexplained. The Top Ten Most Haunted Cemetery or Graveyards, http://www.hauntedamericatours.com/hauntedcemeteries/toptenhauntedcemeteries/

Haunted Wisconsin, Wisconsin Haunted Places, http://www.angelfire.com/psy/sewgr/hauntedwi.html

Haunted Wisconsin Vortexs, Paranormal Hot Spots, Ghosts, UFOs, http://www.burlingtonnews.net/wisconsinvortexs.html

History of the Great Lakes – Wreck of the Lady Elgin, http://www.mfhn.com/glsdb/archivestemp/ldyelgn.html

JS Online, Purported ghosts are frightfully ordinary, http://www2.jsonline.com/news/metro/oct00/nichcol06100500a.asp

Mars Haunted House History, http://marshauntedhouse.com/MarsHauntedHouse/history.html

Milwaukee Area Paranormal Investigations, Haunted Places in Milwaukee, http://www.milwaukeeparanormal.com/Haunted-Places-In-Milwaukee.html

The Shadowlands, Haunted Places in Wisconsin, http://www.theshadowlands.net/places/wisconsin.htm

WIX's Haunted Wisconsin's Database, http://www.hauntedwi.com/WIXhauntedlocations.htm

Wikepedia, Forest Home Cemetery, http://en.wikipedia.org/wiki/Forest_Home_Cemetery

Wikipedia, James Strang http://en.wikipedia.org/wiki/James_Strang

Index